Week by Week

with George Duncan

Pickering & Inglis
LONDON · GLASGOW

DEDICATED TO
MY SIX GRAND-CHILDREN
GEORGE, TIMOTHY, NICOLA,
TANYA, EMILY and ANDREW

ILLUSTRATIONS

*The illustration pages are reproduced
from colour transparencies photographed
by the author on his world-wide travels.*

INTRODUCTION

I am sure that it was both in his love and in his wisdom that our Creator, Redeemer and Father God required of men that they should set apart one day in seven for himself in a rather special way. On that day the Word of God has for so many of us taken a central place. I realise that we are living in days when the place of the sermon is denigrated in some quarters until it has practically disappeared, and in others exalted in such a way that its inordinate length makes it excessively dull and dreary. Both ways of handling it, in my judgment, are wrong. God is never dull, but God always has something to say to men through his Word. When I was vicar at Christ Church, Cockfosters in North London, one of the big London evening papers made a survey of churches that were well attended to find out the reasons for good attendances at some churches and not at others. At that time in Christ Church, we were having to hold two evening services, the numbers were so great. The reporter asked me why I felt that so many people came. I replied that I believed that people wanted to know what God had to say to them, and that all that I tried to do was to find out from the Bible what God wanted to say, and then to say it! That made every Sunday an exciting day for me and I trust for those who in the mercy of God sat under my ministry. This book is a selection of the kind of messages that I have sought to bring to my congregations. As they would seem to have been a help to them, I trust that they may in this condensed form be a help to many more.

Some people are unable to get to church because of advancing years, or because of ill health, others are tied to the home with duties, or prevented from attending church because of their occupation. Many live too far from any church to be able to go regularly, while others, when they do go, find, alas, that instead of being offered the bread of the Word of God, they are given

5

the stone of a man's own thoughts! It is my hope and prayer that into whatever hands this book falls, those who read it may find some light upon the path, some food for their souls, some strength for the battle! It may even be that some, who themselves have the responsibility for feeding the flock, will find inspiration and help in understanding what is one of the most demanding of all tasks, but which, under the blessing and guidance of the Spirit of God, is surely the most rewarding.

I owe an immense debt to so many whose books and ministry have helped me—so many that I cannot even begin to mention names. To them and to those who have prayed for me I would express my gratitude. I hope that the help that I trust will come through the reading of this book will be a reward to them as they realise the help they have been to me. I thank God for the privilege of having been called to 'preach the word'.

G.B.D.

A Time to Act

Now then do it

2 SAMUEL 3:18

'YE sought for David in times past to be king over you, now then do it.' The words were the words of the commander-in-chief of the army of the house of Saul; words which came as a tremendous challenge to the people of Israel and words which reflect the kind of issue that can still confront the hearts of men and women today.

Behind the words there was **disillusionment.** The long years of the reign of the first king of Israel had ended in defeat and dishonour. Abner could no doubt recall *the expectancy with which the reign had commenced.* Saul had been a most attractive young man not only in appearance but in his qualities of character. The only snag seemed to be his almost total inability to understand the ways of God.

The nation of Israel had wanted a king so as to be like the other nations round about them. Abner had no doubt enough sense to realise *the perplexity with which the reign had been marked* as it had dragged on its long weary years. The perplexity in the minds of thinking people as they watched the defeats that had come Saul's way. The hatred with which he had so relentlessly pursued David, the fact that he so obviously did not understand the ways of God.

The whole long sorry story culminated in his defeat at the hands of his enemies, and his death. Disillusionment after such high hopes. The kind of disillusionment that still comes to those who turn their backs upon the rule of God, and seek the seemingly more attractive ways of the world.

Behind the words of Abner we can also see **postponement.** As commander-in-chief of the armies of King Saul, Abner's ear would be close enough to the ground to know what was happening in the mind of the nation. He would know *the direction of the thoughts* of the people. On to the scene had come David with victory and with all the attraction of a man upon whose life obviously the seal of the divine blessing was resting, court favourite, national hero and then for so many years fugitive before the hate of King Saul.

How often the people's thoughts would turn to the man in hiding, wishing that he might be the man on the throne. But if Abner knew the direction of their thought, he also sensed *the diffidence in their hearts.* They would like to have made David King but they dared not do it. Fear of Saul kept them back.

I wonder how often the same condition has existed in the hearts of men and women today. Disillusioned after giving their allegiance to the world with all its fair promise, their thoughts have turned towards David's greater Son, the despised and rejected of men, turned wistfully, almost longingly. What would they not give to have him as Master of their lives, but although the wish has been there, they have done nothing about it.

Behind the words of Abner there was just one more thing. There was **enthronement.** 'Ye sought for David in times past to be king over you, now then do it.' *The meaning was clear.* Already some of the nation had taken the step, Judah had already crowned him; the challenge now came to the rest of the nation to do the thing they had purposed to do for so long. The alternative was the pathetic representative of the house of Saul who had finally, with his foul accusation, shattered for ever any illusion that might have existed in the mind of Abner that better days were ahead with the house of Saul.

The man they were offered was David, the man after God's own heart, *the moment had come*, the moment for action was now. As we find ourselves at the threshold of another year, the same challenge comes to our own hearts, to those of us who have purposed for so long to make Jesus King, but have never done it. 'Ye sought in times past for David's greater Son to be king over you, *now then do it*.'

Would it not be wonderful if for you the New Year could begin with your coronation of him as Lord and Master of your life; you have purposed to do it so often—but you have put off the moment of decision— '*now then do it*'.

Try Love

The love of Christ constraineth us

2 CORINTHIANS 5:14

THIS was the advice of General Booth of the Salvation Army which he cabled out to two workers who had written in to Headquarters speaking of difficulties and discouragements. 'Try love'—it would not be an overstatement to say that most ailments within the church today can be traced to its absence.

'While faith makes all things possible, love makes all things easy' was a dictum of Evan Hopkins, an early and beloved speaker at the Keswick Convention. Here are some thoughts upon Christian love we might do well to ponder.

How love begins: One thing is certain about love and that is that love cannot be 'worked up' and that is a fact the New Testament acknowledges. The New Testament speaks of two aspects of love which are basic to the problem.

There is *the gift of love*: Romans 5:5. 'The love of God is shed abroad in our hearts by the Holy Ghost which is given to us.' Love comes with life. Just as eternal life is a gift—so too is the love which is inseparable from the life.

Indeed one of the evidences of the new life is the new love, e.g. 1 John 3:14, 'We know that we have passed from death into life—because we love . . .' the word of God, the house of God, the will of God, people of God!

There is also *the growth of love*: Philippians 1:9, 'This I pray that your love may abound yet more and more in knowledge'. Love may be there—but it may not be strong. If it is to grow it must be 'in knowledge'—

you cannot love someone you don't know. And this is just the mistake so many Christians are making—they are trying to love a God they don't know and they don't know him because they so seldom spare time to be with him with their Bible open, their knees bent and their will bent too. 'That I may know him' was Paul's ambition. It should be ours.

What love becomes: There are two things that love becomes—there will be more, but let us consider two.

Love becomes *the motive of our service*: e.g. 2 Corinthians 5:14, 'the love of Christ constraineth us'. Love is both tireless in the expenditure of its strength and also thoughtful in its insight of others' need. How definitely the church needs this kind of service. What job so demanding as a mother's task and yet what task more happily fulfilled.

Love becomes *the measure of our surrender*. Love is a great and glad giver. When Paul commands, 'Yield yourselves unto God' (Rom. 6:13)—it is not the submission of love to the threat of the tyrant he has in mind but the glad surrender of love to the plea of a greater love. 'We love him, because he first loved us.'

How love behaves: The New Testament is essentially a practical book and while it puts doctrine first and rightly so, it never fails to put in practice also.

Love will have its *standard for its behaviour*. The first description of this is Paul's own in 1 Corinthians 13:4–7, 'Love is very patient, very kind. Love knows no jealousy: Love makes no parade, gives itself no airs: is never rude: never selfish: never irritated: never resentful: love is never glad when others go wrong: love is gladdened by goodness: always glad to forgive: always eager to believe the best: always hopeful: always patient: always there!' What a standard!

There will be *the sequel to love's behaviour*. 'By this shall all men know that you are my disciples, if ye have love one to another' (John 13:35). We won't have to explain to others that we are Christians, they'll know it without being told—maybe will want to know the Saviour for themselves. TRY LOVE!

Evangelism Defined

Multitudes in the valley of decision

JOEL 3:14

O NE of the simplest and best definitions of evangelism I have ever heard is 'the offering of the whole Christ, by the whole church for the whole man, throughout the whole world', and I would like to add 'for the whole time'. How this lifts evangelism away from that cheap conception of it that some of its opponents have held—with little mental thought or spiritual insight.

The whole Christ. *There is a danger* in all Christian thinking and preaching, the danger of taking and proclaiming only that part of the Christian revelation which appeals to us, or of which we approve. Some folk treat the teaching of Christ as they would a menu card, accepting what they want and leaving the rest.

There is a duty here, the duty incumbent upon all who are called to be witnesses, to speak the truth, the whole truth and nothing but the truth. The Christian church has the duty to proclaim and reveal the whole Christ. In his incarnation, teaching and miracles, his death and resurrection, and in his indwelling and coming again.

The whole church. Offering the whole Christ by the whole church. Think how the Commission was given to the whole church; and *the immensity of the task* demands that everyone be engaged upon it. When everyone is engaged upon the task, the opportunities are multiplied. Think how many lives you touch every week, and then multiply that number by the number of folk in your church and see how many lives can be influenced for Christ in a week.

The diversity of gifts demands that everyone be involved in it. Think of the conception of the church we find in the New Testament as 'the body of Christ', which confirms that this is so. Just as the will of the mind is exercised through our bodies through the harmonious functioning of all its various members, so the redemptive will of God is to be expressed through the church.

The whole man. Here we must note *the area of God's concern.* It is for the whole man—not simply for the saving of his soul—the saving of his life in every aspect, in every relationship and in every activity. The will of God touches man's mind, body and spirit.

Here, we can see, lies *the answer to man's protest* that we should keep religion out of politics; that what happens on Sunday must not interfere with what happens throughout the rest of the week. Whatever affects man for good or ill concerns God.

The whole world. God is not British, although we almost always think he is! *The range of the love of God* covers the world, 'God so loved the world that he gave . . .' So then we must be concerned with the world.

The resources for the work of God are supplied by him. For the one who said 'Ye shall be witnesses unto me unto the uttermost parts of the earth' said also 'Ye shall receive power after that the Holy Ghost is come upon you'.

Are You Dead?

Thou hast a name that thou livest, and art dead

REVELATION 3:1

I WANT to examine a spiritual condition which is, alas, all too common and which is the very antithesis of life. 'Thou hast a name that thou livest, and art dead.' The words were spoken about a church. You will find the story in Revelation 3:1–6. There are three searching thoughts to ponder here.

This was a church in which **spiritual life was assumed.** You see, they had the name, although they did not have the life. Was it not a church? Were they not members of the church?

We must face the fact that *the possibility exists of making such an assumption.* It existed then, therefore it must exist now, and the reason was a simple one, they had the name, a name that was used usually within the limits and confines of the Christian experience.

We have so many names of this kind, member of the church, Sunday school teacher, choir member, churchwarden, deacon, elder, minister, vicar, bishop and so on. But these are all just names which assume spiritual life, they neither bestow it nor convey it. It is not enough to have the name, we must have the life.

We do well too to think of *the tragedy that results from making such an assumption*; the tragedy of disappointment and disillusionment. You may recall how in the early years of our Lord's life his parents lost him, for they set out 'supposing him to have been in the company'.

This was a church from which **spiritual life was absent.** 'Thou hast a name that thou livest, *and art dead.*' This of course follows on from the first. Our Lord here is speaking of a dead church, James speaks of 'a dead faith', Paul speaks of those who are 'dead while they live'. There are two further thoughts worth pondering here.

Consider *the stillness that reigns in death*. There is an awesome stillness, a lack of any movement, when death comes. So it was here. Not that the church was without its 'works', but in the realm of that which was distinctly spiritual there was neither life nor movement.

Consider also *the sickness that results from death*. There is an infection as well as an inaction in death. When any great disaster, like an earthquake, hits a town, the one fear is that an epidemic will follow. Our Lord speaks here of those 'things which are ready to die'. When death comes to a church, then the very environment in which life once existed begins to suffer. The services of the church, the standards of the Christian, the practices of devotion, the Lord's Day, the infection spreads and endangers them.

This was a church to which **spiritual life was available.** Christ speaks as the one that 'hath the seven spirits of God'. The number 'seven' denotes perfection or completeness, the 'Spirits' speak of life. The church which is dead must face two demands.

It must face the fact that the answer to death is life, and that the way to life is through birth. *The miracle of spiritual birth* is the offer of Christ through the Holy Spirit. 'Ye must be born' spiritually, was Christ's word to Nicodemus. Every generation needs to face this demand, every individual.

The second demand lies in *the measure of spiritual life* offered by the One who has the 'seven spirits of God'. This is abundant life, fulness of life, life that is life indeed, life that is none other than the life of the risen Christ mediated through the Holy Spirit. God grant that we who have the name, may have the life too.

Know Your Enemy

Your adversary the devil
1 PETER 5:8

IN every realm of life we should know our enemies. In the field of health there are those factors which endanger our health and these are studied and taken into account. In sport, the would-be victor will study his opponents so that he may overthrow them. In the wider issues of war, rival armies will study one another, so as to gain victory. But in the realm of the soul how little thought the average Christian gives to the enemy.

When we turn to the Bible there are three facts we should note about him. The first concerns **his purpose to discredit.** In Revelation 12:10, we read of him as the accuser of the brethren. *The attack we must face* may be a direct one upon the conscience, overwhelming the Christian with a sense of his own unworthiness, depressing and discouraging him out of the service of Jesus Christ, and out of his assurance of salvation and acceptance before God. Or the attack may come indirectly through the lips of other Christians, or the world that criticises the measure of failure evident in his life. Most of us must have known this side of the enemy of our souls, and felt discouraged almost to the point of admitting defeat.

Is there *an answer that we can give* to this accuser? There is a very old and a complete one. We can overcome him 'by the blood of the Lamb'. Never at any time is the Christian accepted before God because of his righteousness. Saved by Grace, we are to continue to 'stand in grace'.

To move off that ground is to throw our lives wide open to the attack of the accuser, to remain there is to remain on ground where he cannot come. To his

Top—Flamboyant Poinciana ▶
Bottom—By the shore, Loch Lomond

foulest and truest taunts we have one answer, 'the blood of the Lamb which cleanses from all stain and sin'.

The Bible speaks also of the enemy's **plan to deceive.** In Revelation 12:9, we read of him as one 'which deceiveth the whole world', and in another Scripture we read that he was a liar from the beginning. How clever his approach can be—veiled in language which professes a concern for our happiness, it can be accompanied by the fairest of promises but *marked by deceit!* Was that not the approach he made to our first parents in the Garden of Eden? 'Hath God said ye shall not eat of every tree?' 'In the day ye eat thereof ye shall be as Gods', 'Ye shall not surely die'.

It has been said that in war, truth is the first casualty. It is certainly so in the spiritual warfare. There is only one answer to deceit, and that is truth. We have that in the word of God, the truth about sin, the truth about happiness, the truth about ourselves and so he can be *met with defeat.* How vital it is that every Christian should be steeped in the word of God so that we are not deceived by the enemy.

From the Bible we also learn of **his power to destroy.** In 1 Peter 5:8, we read of him 'as a roaring lion walking about seeking whom he may devour'. *The strength of the enemy* must not be underestimated and the Christian is foolish indeed who thinks that he is himself competent to deal with such a foe. None of us would relish facing a lion unarmed and alone. Thank God we need not face the devil thus. What, or who, is *the source of our victory?* Like the old negro who was taunted by his master after his conversion we cannot say we have the mastery of the devil, but 'we hab de Master ob de devil'. In the power of the risen life of our indwelling Lord we have the One before whom even he must bow.

Special Messenger

The Lord's messenger in the Lord's message
HAGGAI 1:13

IT would be interesting to find out just what the average person expects the minister or vicar to be like. I suppose he ought to have the bedside manner of a doctor, the voice of a BBC announcer, the skin of a rhinoceros, the patience of a Job, the strength of an ox and the personality and figure of a film star! There is a verse in the Bible which is possibly even more demanding; it describes one such man as 'the Lord's messenger in the Lord's message'. A phrase worth thinking over. It tells us at least three things about such a man.

Firstly, he will be **fashioned by its truth.** In this aspect of his life and work there will be two important considerations. In the first place, *the truth must be learned* by him. He must learn what the Lord's message is if he is to declare and deliver it. He is a messenger, not just a preacher, he is an 'ambassador for Christ' whose task is to say what he is told.

He will always be learning the truth. There can be no greater tragedy in the life of any minister than when he stops learning. His message has to do with the unsearchable riches of Christ, so he ought not to run out of subject matter. He should always be creative and never simply repetitive.

But *the truth must be lived* by him. He is the 'Lord's messenger *in* the Lord's message'. That suggests that the truth of God is to be the environment, the very breath of his Christian life. The truth is not simply to be learned, it must be lived. His life is to be the expression of the message he preaches. 'Truth through personality' is the classic definition of preaching, and as that truth passes through that personality so the personality must be adjusted to the truth.

Secondly, 'The Lord's messenger in the Lord's message' will be **fragrant from its touch.** Two modern translations help us here. Moffatt's translation of 2 Corinthians 2:14 and Phillips': '. . . he makes my life a constant pageant of triumph in Christ, diffusing the perfume of his knowledge everywhere by me,' and 'Thanks be to God who makes our knowledge of him to spread throughout the whole world like a lovely perfume.'

This will be due to *the infection that fellowship brings.* The fragrance is inherently Christ's, but through the closeness of his contact with him that fragrance becomes his! Just as linen sheets put away with lavender catch its fragrance, so the life that is lived close to Christ catches the very fragrance of Christ.

There will also be *the attraction that fragrance gives.* A lovely perfume is arresting. There should be something arresting and attractive about the whole character of a minister of the gospel.

Finally, 'the Lord's messenger in the Lord's message' will be **forgotten in its telling.** Fashioned by its truth, fragrant from its touch and forgotten in its telling. I have heard of a church in which there were two texts designed to catch the eye of the preacher. The first he saw as he went into the pulpit, 'Sir, we would see Jesus', and the second as he left, 'They saw no man save Jesus only'.

We must not ignore *the place of personality* in the work of the ministry, or the fact that God uses different personalities to reach different people.

But we must not ignore *the peril of personality.* The task of the preacher is never to attract people to himself or to his preaching but to his Lord. He is after all only the 'Lord's messenger in the Lord's message'.

> 'I ask thee not for subtle thought,
>   For picture exquisitely wrought,
> For speech or grand or graceful turn,
>   For tones that thrill and words that burn,
> Let me but touch thy garment's hem,
>   and bear the fragrance unto them.'

Christians Speak Up

Let the redeemed of the Lord say so

PSALM 107:2

T HERE'S a verse in the Bible which says 'Let the redeemed say so'. Would a modern translation be, 'Let Christians speak up'? How far is your faith vocal, or do you share in the conspiracy of silence that seems to have fallen upon evangelical and protestant Christianity.

When reading *Turbulent Journey*, the biography of Lloyd George, I noticed how respect had to be paid to what was called 'the conscience of nonconformity'. Today one wonders if any respect has to be paid to Christian conscience at all.

Think of **the difficulties of speaking up.** It will mean sometimes taking the trouble to write a letter. Have you ever written a letter to the BBC either expressing appreciation or criticism of their programmes? Or are you too lazy? It means taking a lead and that's not easy.

It means being willing to face *criticism* and even hatred from the world. We are told to expect that, but most of us shirk it. We want to be acceptable with the world that crucified our Lord. It could mean loneliness. And none of us like that. It demands *courage* and most of us are bigger cowards than we like to think.

It demands being true to what we know to be right, and the majority of Christians prefer to compromise with truth and right when it suits their own convenience. It is no easy task being a witness, but a witness must speak up, and that is the task to which we are called, 'Ye shall be witnesses'. What then are we to think of **the duty of speaking up?** If the world presents something in the realm of entertainment, or literature and labels it excellent, when, judged by Christian standards, it is foul, is the Christian to remain silent?

One of the tragedies of today is the refusal of Christians to think, and then for them to speak out. The *testimony we must bear to the world* demands that we speak up. Not that we must do it rudely or unreasonably, but that we do it.

The *opportunity we must give to the world* demands that we speak up! How else is the world to know? The cry from the New Testament rings out 'How shall they hear without a preacher?' and a preacher must surely speak. Have you done any preaching recently?

What then is to be **the dynamic for speaking up?** *From whence does the power come?* In this, as in every other task of the Christian, the power is to be divine. The cleverness of our reasoning, the eloquence of our pleading, the logic of our arguing, the facts of our case, these in themselves are not enough to convict men of sin, it is the work of the Holy Spirit alone to do that, and therefore we come back, as always in the work and witness of the Christian church, to our relationship to Christ.

Through whom will the power flow? The man who will do great things for God is the one who is living rightly related to him. Those who have read the memoirs of Montgomery will realise that the secret of the victories that marked his career lay in part in the fact that he never fought until he was sure that the conditions for victory had been fulfilled. Let us never take the Holy Spirit for granted, but once we have sought in humility to be right with God, then for Christ's sake and for the world's sake, let the Christian speak up.

Words that Wound

Set a watch, O Lord, before my mouth

PSALM 141:3

THE Bible never underestimates the importance
of the words we utter. In the New Testament,
in the epistle of James, the right use of words is
taken as a guide to our spiritual maturity. In Proverbs
12:18 we are reminded 'There is that speaketh like the
piercings of a sword'. Words are constantly on our lips,
in the home, where we work, with our friends, with our
enemies. How careless we so often are about them.

Let us think through this thought suggested by
these words in Proverbs for a moment. There are three
truths that immediately leap to mind when we think
about 'words that wound'.

Think of **the depth that may vary.** Some words
may *wound slightly*. Some wounds are superficial, mere
scratches and therefore possibly not of so much
significance to our minds. Some words will *wound
deeply*. Is this not true of words spoken or written?
Some may hurt us only very slightly, others seem to go
deep down into our very souls. It may often be that the
wound is deeper than we think.

Think of **the dirt that can gather.** This is true
physically of the body. This is why even a slight wound
may be a serious wound, not because of the depth to it
but because of the dirt in it. We all have heard cases of
tiny scratches that have led to serious illness.

But it is also true *spiritually!* Resentment,
bitterness, unforgiveness, doubt, all these and much
more besides can gather in a wound made by words.
What we said may have seemed of such little
importance to us. Indeed we may have scarcely noticed
and certainly have not remembered what we said or

22

wrote, but the wound, though slight, was an opening into which dirt came and brought disablement with it.

Think of **the death that may ensue.** This does happen in the physical realm. We must have heard of incidents when even a tiny scratch has sometimes resulted in death. It is true in the spiritual realm also. Words can do much more than wound; they can kill. They can kill a person's zeal for Christ; they can kill a person's faith in God; they can kill a person's desire to become a Christian. Yes, death may be the result of words that wound.

There seem to be two things, then, that we must do about words. The first concerns *the words,* we must not speak words that wound, and we shall be more careful if we have given thought to what the Bible has to say about them. The second concerns *the wounds,* we must not let dirt gather in the wounds. Bring the wounds to the cleansing forgiveness of Jesus.

Seek forgiveness and confess the sin that would fain come into the wound, be it slight or deep, and know the cleansing of the blood of Christ. We would do well to pray constantly the prayer of the psalmist; 'Keep the door of my lips, Set a watch, O Lord, before my mouth.'

Better than Sacrifice

Whatsoever he saith unto you, do it

JOHN 2:5

I REMEMBER hearing a talk on the 'whatsoevers' of the Christian life, and amongst them, 'Whatsoever he saith unto you, do it' as 'the whatsoever of Christian obedience'. Most of us would agree that the main problem in the life of the church is not related to the truth we do not know, but to our obedience to the truth we do already know.

I think the root and heart of God's problem is that simple but urgent lesson which our parents found very difficult to instil into us when we were small, when they would say again and again 'when will you learn to do as you are told?' It may be that God does not want to teach you anything new, but he does want you to become obedient to his will in whatsoever respect his will has been revealed to you. May I then bring to you the thought and truth and challenge of the need for obedience in the Christian life?

First, **in our obedience lies the very purpose of our redemption by God.** You may ask, 'Why has God saved me?' God has saved you in order that you may be obedient to him. In 1 Peter 1:2 we find that clearly stated: 'Elect according to the foreknowledge of God the Father, through sanctification of the Spirit, *unto obedience . . .*'

We are elected unto obedience. The whole purpose of God could be summed up in this one word. Obedience involves, first of all, *an acceptance of God's way of redemption*. Peter goes on to say 'Elect . . . unto obedience and sprinkling of the blood of Jesus Christ.' What way are you following in order to find acceptance with God? Are you relying upon your church membership? Upon the sacraments? Upon your righteousness or decency, or family, or upbringing? None of these avails. There is only one way; Christ.

When we come to Christ we are led to the Cross! The first obedience that God asks of us is that we be ready to accept the way of redemption that he has provided. You do not have to make yourself right with God. It is a work that is done. It was completed by our Lord on the Cross and now it has only got to be accepted. Have you been obedient to that? Are you trusting in the death of Christ for your salvation?

Acceptance of God's way of salvation will lead to *an acceptance of God's will in life*. The mark of a Christian is that he or she will do what God wants. Can you say that your only desire in life is to know God's will and then to do it, at whatever cost?

In our obedience lies the pathway to our experience of God. In the history of the church there is no question of the reality of the experience of God! God's children know that prayer is not just talking into space. Why is it then that for so many the experience is almost nil? There is *an experiment that faith must make*. There is a revealing phrase in the story of the healing of the lepers by our Lord, in Luke 17:14 'As they went they were cleansed'. The experience of the healing power of Christ did not come to them until they were obedient. He said 'Go', and 'as they went they were cleansed'.

There is then *the experience that faith will have*. Obedience is the gateway to our experience of God.

You may have been spiritually stuck for weeks, for months, for years, and you know where you got stuck—at the place where you became disobedient to the will of God. You never yielded to God on that point, and spiritually you have not gone one step further.

In our obedience lies the proof of our devotion to God. In John 14:21, we read 'He that hath my commandments and keepeth them, he it is that loveth me'; and in chapter 15:14, 'Ye are my friends, if ye do whatsoever I command you'. Oh, *the substitutes* that you and I try to find for obedience! Do you judge your keenness as a Christian by your place in the life of the church? You say 'I am a Deacon, a Sidesman, a Sunday school teacher, I am in the choir.' None of this proves your devotion to Christ.

The proof of our devotion to God lies in the measure of our obedience.

You will remember the searching words of the prophet to King Saul, 'Hath the Lord as great delight in burnt offerings and sacrifices as in obeying the voice of the Lord? Behold, to obey is better than sacrifice.' This is *the standard* we must accept in our lives!

Can you imagine the transformation that would happen in the life of your church fellowship and mine if every professing Christian showed the proof of his professed devotion to God, in a life of simple, true and complete obedience? 'Whatsoever he saith unto you, do it.' In our obedience lies the purpose of our redemption by God, the pathway to our experience of God, and the proof of our devotion to God.

The Task of Meditation

Thou shalt meditate
JOSHUA 1:8

I N God's commission to Joshua He included as one
of the essentials for success that Joshua should allow
time every day for the task of meditation.

When tackling a task, the first requirement is **the
gathering of tools.**

Many people fail in the task of meditation because
they fail to do this.

We could divide the tools into two categories;
first, the *essentials*—a good Bible and a quiet place.

Some people handicap themselves by having a
Bible with a very small type. Every Christian should get
a really good Bible, preferably with a wide margin.
These are specially produced with paper that will take
ink and although they are, naturally, a little bulky for
carrying around, they are invaluable to keep at home. I
know a church that gives one to every new missionary
sent out to the field.

The quiet place is equally essential. Our Lord said
'When thou prayest . . . shut the door.'

Extra tools you will find valuable include pen and
pencil. You can use different colours to underline
important verses—red for sin and salvation—green, the
Christian life—blue, prophecy and heaven, and black for
making notes in the margin.

In this way we can mark, record and remember
what we learn from our meditation of God's Word.

Extra tools also include modern translations. The
value of these translations lies in their clarity. To read a
passage in a modern translation before going back to the
Authorised Version often gives a clear understanding of
its meaning. Other books of devotion also have their

place and value to stimulate our minds and heart but these must never take the place of the Bible itself.

From what I have said you will realise that the task of meditation involves **the giving of time.** Most people suffer from the speed at which we live. This applies particularly to our life of communion with God. We need *time for God* to reveal his thoughts to us. Just as in our friendships we don't reveal the depths of our thoughts and hearts to the casual stranger who chats to us for a few minutes, neither does God reveal the deep things of the Spirit to the casual Christian who drops in for a chat. The pages of the Bible seem to be overlaid with a thin film which obscures their real meaning, and it is only with the wearing away of this film through constant use that the real meaning is at last laid bare!

We also need *time to prove* our sincerity to God. Indications in the Bible are clear that God has no time for triflers. It is those who really hunger and thirst after righteousness who are filled. It is those who are pure in heart that see God, and time is a proof of sincerity.

But finally the task of meditation will mean **the gleaning of truth.** Every Christian should be learning steadily and daily from the Word itself the truth of God, and yet so many Christians seem to learn so little this way. They depend almost entirely on sermons they hear, or books they read. In the gleaning of truth from the Word of God first *analyse the text*, break up into sections the passage or the verse, so as to realise all the Scripture has to say. Secondly, *crystalise the truth*, put it into a sentence or series of sentences so as to remember what God wishes us to learn. It is this final conclusion that I record either in the wide margin of my Bible or in a notebook.

Just as God included the task of meditation in his commission to Joshua, so all down the centuries you will find that wherever true and deep success has marked any Christian life, hidden away in a secret place there has been faithfulness in fulfilling the task of daily meditation.

They Watched Him There

Sitting down they watched him there
MATTHEW 27:36

ONCE at least every year the story of the Cross will be told through radio, television, church services throughout the world as Easter draws near.

Sitting down we shall watch him there.

How differently the eyes of men looked upon the Redeemer in his dying love. **The eyes of the wicked** watched him there! What shall we say of the Scribes and Pharisees, who had hounded him to his death; of Pontius Pilate, who through cowardice had sent him there?

Did Pilate, I wonder, make his way out to that desolate hill, wrapped up in a cloak, his face hidden, that none might recognise him, so that he too standing afar off watched him there? What were *the motives in their hearts?*

In Pilate's heart it was fear of man, in the hearts of the Scribes and Pharisees it was love of position, and possession. Cowardice and hypocrisy, fear and greed. Grim and terrible forces, that led these wicked men to reject Christ, but let us beware lest in condemning them we condemn ourselves. What was *the meaning of the Cross?*

The Cross meant to them the disposal of the righteousness by which they themselves were condemned.

To them the Cross was the end, the destruction of the righteousness, goodness and holiness which was Christ's.

We too live in a world where men are prepared to stand by, indeed to plan for the elimination of that which they know to be right. As they look on the Cross its meaning for them is the same. They would rather see righteousness destroyed than lose their wealth. To them Christ is dead, and they are glad.

The eyes of the wondering also watched him there. How many there must have been baffled and perplexed by the Cross. I think of *the Roman soldiers* who were no fools. They had carried out many sentences, but never such a travesty of justice as this. They thought of Barabbas, the prisoner they had released, and then thought of Christ. They had seen his ministry of healing, heard the prisoner pronounced 'Not Guilty', 'Behold, I find no fault in him at all', and yet he was hanging there.

I think too of *the little children*. A city had witnessed two processions in the space of a week, the one coming into the city with rejoicing, the one going forth, the Redeemer bearing his Cross. How bewildered the children must have been. Why were men crucifying their Saviour and friend. Why were those hands that so often had blessed them nailed to this cruel stake?

Why was that face, so often lit with a rare radiancy as he smiled upon them, now bespattered with spittle and blood? The eyes of the wondering watched him there.

But finally **the eyes of the worshipping** watched him. There were at least two who *saw the real person on the Cross*, the thief who had the faith to see that Christ was a King, 'Lord remember me when thou comest into thy kingdom,' and the officer of the guard who cried out 'Truly this was the Son of God.'

But was there another watcher there who sensed *the real purpose of the Cross*, the man standing afar off half hidden by the bushes with the tears streaming down his face? Never would he forget that day. As the first streak of dawn lit the walls of his prison cell, he had looked out into the prison yard to see there the three stakes, one of which was his, and the one that had been his now bore the body of the dying Lord. Was

Barabbas that man? Did he sense the purpose as well as see the person of Christ? Christ was dying because he meant to die, not because men had taken him and nailed him there, but because his life and the passion of God for men took him to that death that there he might bear in his own body the sins of the world.

The Third Day He Rose Again

He is not here, but is risen

LUKE 24:6

THE truth of the rising again from the dead of Jesus Christ lies at the very heart of the Christian faith. Look at this tremendous truth within the setting of the New Testament. Three facts emerge.

The resurrection was predicted in the ministry of Christ. Long before it happened it was talked about. *It was recorded in the sayings of Jesus.* To take one gospel only, Matthew's, we find references to it on at least four different occasions. In Matthew 12:39–40, when certain of the scribes asked for a sign; in Matthew 16: 21, on the occasion of Peter's confession that Jesus was the Christ; in Matthew 17:23, not long after his transfiguration; in Matthew 20:17–19, on their way to Jerusalem for the last time. The resurrection was as clearly in the mind of Christ as the crucifixion!

It was recalled by the enemies of Jesus. In Matthew 27:62, 63, we read how, after the crucifixion, they said, 'Sir, we . . . remember that that deceiver said while he was yet alive, after three days I will rise again.'

It is one aspect of this stupendous event that has to be taken into account, that it was predicted and expected both by Jesus Christ and his enemies. The guard at the tomb, the ropes, the seal, all these must be explained away if this were not so.

The resurrection was presented as a miracle of God. A miracle for which the only explanation is to be found in God himself and his almighty power. All

32   *Top*—A quiet corner of Lake Derwentwater
          Bottom—The front at Eastbourne ▶

four gospels tell the story and concerning these records it is worthwhile noting two aspects.

The details in the descriptions. It is maintained by some that as the details apparently do not tally therefore the records must be false. But anyone with experience of examining eye-witnesses knows how much variation there may be in detail, but that there is also an emerging stratum of fact common to all accounts.

We have in each account the empty grave, the terror of the guards, the amazement of the disciples, the appearance of the Master, the message of the angels. Basically, the stories are the same, and carry all the vividness of the language of eye-witnesses.

The difficulties in its denial. To deny the resurrection is to raise even greater difficulties than to accept it. How otherwise is the transformation of the disciples to be accounted for? Why was not the body produced to make their preaching the nonsense it would then have been? The very church itself depends on the resurrection, and that must then be explained away, too.

The resurrection was proclaimed in the message of the church. Whether we examine the preaching of Peter or of Paul, the crucifixion of Jesus and his rising again are the central themes. The resurrection was preached with a twofold stress. *It was preached* as *the seal and vindication of Christ's work*—as something which God had done, and by which he set his own divine seal on the validity and authority of the words and work of Christ. *It was preached as the secret and victory of the Christian experience.* Through the resurrection a new quality of life was made available here and now for the Christian to enjoy (Phil. 3:10), and also in the resurrection an assurance was given of the certainty of a life to come hereafter (1 Cor. 15:20). 'Alive for evermore' is true not only of Christ but of the Christian who shares his risen and victorious life. Hallelujah!

Transformed

The two disciples heard him . . . and followed Jesus

JOHN 1:37

THE Bible is a fascinating book in that its stories illustrate the spiritual experiences of men and women today. One of the loveliest stories is that of the introduction given by John the Baptist to two of his disciples on the never-to-be-forgotten day when they were introduced to Jesus Christ.

Note **the contact they had with Christ.** These two men would possibly not have made contact with Jesus Christ unless first of all they had known John the Baptist, *they knew John.* How many of us would have to say the same thing, 'I would never have met Christ unless I had known So-and-So.'

These men were John's disciples. They had no doubt been arrested by the ruggedness of his character, the reality of his faith. This man's religion seemed to live! Anyway they listened to him, and studied him, and they gradually made the discovery that his message was not of himself, but of Another.

They knew John, and one day *they saw Jesus.* Having heard John, they followed Jesus. We too have known what it is to be arrested by another; their way of life has been different and gradually we have come to realise that their secret too lay in Another. Can we ever forget the day when we made the discovery that that Other was none other than the living Christ? We too, having known someone, have seen Christ.

Note further **the chance they got from Jesus Christ.** We read that Jesus turned. *He saw* them following. Is there a hint of timidity that lay behind their following?

But 'Jesus saw them following'. If there is any uncertainty about their timidity there is none about their opportunity, for we read that 'Jesus turned', and that implies that *he stopped*. Is it not wonderfully true that God gives every man his chance; that day when we come face to face with the fact, the truth and the person of the Christ of God? Has such a day come to you? Is this the day?

Note **the challenge they faced in Christ.** 'Jesus saith unto them,' and in that word spoken by Christ to these men lay the challenge. At the heart of any vital Christian experience lies the fact that God speaks to us. The challenge then, as now, was a threefold one.

Christ wanted to save them from three things. First, *the danger of generalities*. 'What seek ye?' How many of us are content with generalities in the sphere of religion. We believe in God but never think through that faith to its logical implications. We say we are Christians but have never taken time to think out what are the specific marks of a true Christian.

The second danger that Christ wanted to save them from was *the danger of delay*. Their reply to his words was as if to say, 'Tell us where you stay, so that we can come some time and talk things over.' Christ's reply was 'Come, and come now'. It might well be that God has put this book into your hands so that you might face up to your decision and reach it today.

But also Christ wanted to save them from *the danger of disillusionment*. He not only said 'come', but 'come *and see*'. These men had been part of a great spiritual movement that was popular and had drawn the crowds. I think Christ wanted them to know that they were in for something far tougher than that, and that he led them away up some lonely glen where he could let them see the loneliness of the way he trod, and speak to them of the costliness of the way they would have to tread.

The final point to note in the story is **the conviction they reached about Christ.** After they had spent that night with Christ they went off with the conviction burned into their very souls, 'we have found

35

the Christ'. The One who was the answer to all their problems and the realisation of all their hopes. *The secret* of that conviction lay in the experience they had of being in his presence, hearing his voice and his word.

That experience can be our experience still today. The secret of their conviction lay there; *the sharing* of it led them forth into a life of telling others what they themselves had discovered. Are you telling others of a Christ whom you have discovered? If not, then have you ever really found him?

The Prayer that Jesus Didn't Pray

Father, save me . . . Father, glorify thy name
JOHN 12:27, 28

I WONDER how many of us have been truly blessed through the reading of the lessons in a church service? Or has that been the moment when you have felt that you could relax and let your mind wander? Many years ago I sat in a church listening to the New Testament lesson being read. The passage was John 12:20–28.

Suddenly while the 27th and 28th verses were being read I found myself jerked awake. I saw two prayers contained within the space of the two verses, one was suggested, only to be rejected, the other was offered! The circumstances surrounding the incident were suggestive and challenging. May I share these thoughts about them with you?

We have here **a soul that was troubled!** 'Now is my soul troubled!' The mind of Christ was troubled at that moment, just as your mind and mine may be troubled as we face our future, even as Christ faced his future. Think of *the suffering entailed* in the future for him. The coming of the Greeks to see him would seem to have brought the Cross into sharp and sudden focus.

The path for the Master was going to be a desperately hard one to tread. Think again of *the solitude entailed* in the future. This path he was to tread in the will of God was one he would have to tread alone. None could share it with him. And when the time came, those who might have helped him by their prayers failed him. How many of us face a path the mere thought of which troubles our minds.

37

We have here **a heart that was tempted.**
'Troubled, and what shall I say, Father save me from
this hour!?' How often that prayer has been the one that
has come almost instinctively to our lips. 'Father save
me from this . . .' Have you ever prayed that prayer?
Have you ever been tempted to do it?

Note two things about that prayer. It would have
been *a selfish prayer.* Save ME! To offer that prayer is
to see no further than ourselves; and life for me as a
child of God involves much more than myself. There is
my world, and there is the glory of my Lord. It would
have been *a stupid prayer.*

In the light of all that was at stake what a tragedy
if it had been prayed and if it had been answered! I
wonder how much loss there has come to the church
because we have prayed just that kind of prayer.

We have here **a love that was trusted.** 'But for
this cause came I unto this hour . . . Father, glorify
Thy name.' What a depth of trust and confidence lies
behind that one word 'Father' as it falls from the lips of
the Son of God. But *how impossible the request.* It
seemed mad to ask that God's name should be glorified
through the Cross.

Have you not felt that some things are just as
impossible in your life? *How immediate the response.* 'I
have and I will . . .' and the whole witness of the
church down the centuries ever since has been part of
the answer. How much God has wrought just because
Jesus didn't pray the prayer that you and I so often
do . . . 'Father save me from this . . .' How much more
God will yet do if we too refuse to pray that prayer and
pray like Jesus 'Father, glorify thy name'.

Mothers at Church

They brought young children to him

MARK 10:13

AS I look back over my ministry the Mothering Sunday services are amongst my happiest memories. What a thrill it is to see so many mothers in church with their children, receiving from their children's hands the posies of spring flowers that are the mothers' gift that day. So I want to think with you about a mother's part in bringing her children to Christ.

It has been said somewhat cynically but, alas, very truly, that when our Lord was on earth mothers brought their children to Jesus; now they send them. Of course, we cannot bring our children to a visible Christ but we can still bring our children to the Master, and I want to leave these thoughts with you together with the prayer that every mother reading them may bring her children to the Saviour in these three simple ways.

First, we can bring our children **in our arms.** Most mothers still have an instinctive desire for God's blessing upon their little ones when they are born, and so they bring them to church either to a service of Holy Baptism or of Dedication. What lies behind these services? First there is *the assurance of a relationship* between God and our little ones, a relationship of love and concern, of interest and desire. 'Ye perceive how by his outward gesture and deed he declared his good will toward them, for he embraced them in his arms, he laid his hands upon them and blessed them. Doubt ye not, therefore, but earnestly believe that he will likewise favourably receive this present infant.'

But also, bringing our little people in our arms, there is *the acceptance of a responsibility.* God assures us

39

of his desire to save, but parents and godparents must accept the responsibility of teaching children to know and love the Saviour. God's desire to save our children does not set aside the need for their decision, and so what happens in church can only be 'until they come of age to take it upon themselves'.

We can bring our children in our arms, but more than that, we can bring them to Christ **on our knees.** Many years ago in my father's church in Edinburgh I heard John McNeill, the great Scottish evangelist, preach. I have forgotten almost everything he said except how he recalled hearing the voice of his mother as she prayed for him in her room after putting him to bed.

This suggests *a priority we must assert.* So many people say they have no time to pray, but it is not true. We must learn to dismiss the multitudes of duties and tasks that clamour for our attention in order to give ourselves to prayer.

But there is also the thought of *a tragedy we must avert.* The tragedy that our children should grow up unprayed for. There is no greater tragedy.

There is one other way in which we can bring our children to Jesus Christ, and that is **by our side.** I was never sent to Sunday School by my parents, but I was always taken to church, and I never cease to be thankful to God for this, and I believe with all my heart that family worship is one of the great needs today.

But in this connection we must remember *the sensitiveness a child will always possess.* We must be careful about the church to which we take our children, otherwise we may given them an impression of God and the things of God which they will never forget and which may put them off church-going for the rest of their lives. But most children will go happily to a living church where the warmth of God's love is felt like the warmth of sunshine. Some parents who are most particular about the school their children go to do not seem to show anything like the same concern about the church.

And finally if we do bring our children to Christ

by our side then we will avoid *the struggle a child should never have*, that struggle between natural affection and spiritual loyalty. I do not know any more pathetic sight than parents who never darken the door of a church and yet send their children to Sunday School, seemingly oblivious to the struggle that begins in the minds of their children as they grow older, between love for their parents and a desire to be with them, and their love for Christ and a desire to be with him. If a family worships together that struggle never comes because the children are able to satisfy both their natural affection and spiritual loyalty. The Roman Church coined a striking motto when it said, 'The family that prays together stays together.'

Will mothers reading these words make a resolve that they will be amongst those who bring their children to Christ in their arms, on their knees, and by their side?

Up Against Things

All these things are against me

GENESIS 42:36

THERE can come a time in any life when we feel we are 'up against things'. The Bible story to read at such a time is the story of Jacob, who felt the same way at the time when, all unknown to him, his son Joseph was ruling one of the greatest empires the world has ever seen.

Jacob put his feelings into these words, 'all these things are against me'. You find the words in Genesis 42:36. It is a lovely story. Read it again if you have not read it for some time. As I read it, it seemed to me that three things marked the experience of Jacob that may mark your experience too.

I can see bitterness here. The words of Jacob were bitter words and understandably so. Think of *the tragedy of his sorrow*. There had been the apparent death of his favourite son Joseph and now this demand that Benjamin, his other favourite son, should go to Egypt where Simeon, another son, was being held as a ransom.

As I listen to the words 'all these things are against me' I realise that there is nothing in life so hurtful as the sorrows which involve our children and our affections.

Is there bitterness in the heart of some reader of these words and the bitterness is because of some hurt in which your child is involved?

Think again of *the threat to his success*. It was a time of terrible famine and Jacob had built up a successful business in herds and cattle, the very existence of which was now threatened. It is always hard to see the results of all our labour disintegrate before our eyes through no fault of our own. Bitterness! Do you know something of this?

I can see blindness here. Can you? As we read the story more carefully we can note *the factor that was ignored* by Jacob. That factor was God. Jacob was so shut up to his problem that he had shut out his God. Not so with Joseph, his much godlier son. Joseph's trials had been even more severe, but as he assessed them he found God at their very heart, and bore this testimony to his brothers. 'It was not you . . . but God.'

Jacob couldn't see God at that moment. There are always two ways of looking at life. Either we look at God through life or we look at life through God.

There is also here *the future that was secured*. God had made certain promises long ago (Gen. 28:13, 14). The present moment might be difficult, but there was no ground for despair as long as the promises remained. Are there not some promises upon which you can rest your faith?

I can see blessedness here. 'All these things are against me.' How wrong you were, Jacob. What was really happening was for your good and the good of your children. *A new integrity in the family was planned.* There was something very wrong in that home and it had never been put right. The brothers had been living a lie for years. God wanted to deal with that and clear up the mess. The brothers realised this when they confessed their sin, 'God hath found out the iniquity of thy servants' (Gen. 44:16).

Also *a new prosperity was planned*, under a new authority. The tribes were no longer to be wanderers but they were to settle in Egypt under the rule of Joseph and become stronger and wealthier than they had ever been. Is God planning something really big in your life? You too have been saying 'all these things are against me'.

How wrong you are!

Do You Care?

Jesus . . . was moved with compassion

MATTHEW 14:14

ONE of the things recorded about Jesus Christ again and again was that he was 'moved with compassion', or 'he had compassion'. To put it more simply 'he cared'. This is all in keeping with the great truth set out in John 3:16, 'God so loved the world that he gave'. But the implications of this are seldom faced by the Christian today.

Our Lord said 'As the Father hath sent me into the world even so send I you'. If he was sent not only to redeem the world but also to reveal the Father, then you and I, if we are Christians, are sent also to reveal the Christ. If caring was a part of his character, it should be a part of ours.

Think then of **the heart that compassion fills.** If compassion is to be shown, then a person is needed through whom this will be done. There must be someone somewhere who cares. *The realities of human need* will have been faced. In Matthew 14:14 we read 'Jesus went forth and saw a great multitude and was moved with compassion toward them.' It was the awareness of the need that aroused his compassion; physical need, spiritual need.

Never was there a day when we were so informed of human need, but do we care? The realities of human need must be met with *the resources of divine love*. As Christ revealed the love of God, so by the indwelling of his Spirit in the lives of believers he seeks to release that same divine love through his church. With the advent of the life of the Spirit, there comes the love of the Spirit (Rom. 5:5).

Think further of **the hands that compassion needs.** Compassion not only feels, it acts. In Matthew 20:34 we read of two blind men upon whom our Lord had compassion, but it did not stop there, 'He touched their eyes'. This comes out again and again, in Mark 1:14; in Luke 10:33; in Luke 7:13.

There is *an activity that compassion demands*. Love is never content to remain idle. Love must act. For the compassion of the Christian there is a whole variety of ways in which this compassion can express itself, through prayer, giving, witnessing, serving, going, etc.

There is also *an identity that compassion desires*. If love never wants to remain idle, it never wants to remain aloof. So often the compassion of the Saviour led to the touch of love, as if to say 'I am here, I am with you'. What about your hands? Are they idle, do you remain aloof or are you involved in the world's cares and needs?

Think finally of **the hope that compassion brings.** Compassion cares, acts and saves. There is *the loneliness that compassion ends*. How desperately lonely some folk are, and depressed because of this. No one else seems to care.

And if the church of Christ doesn't care, then how are they to know that Christ himself cares? Through the touch of your hands they can come to feel the touch of his hands.

The loveliness compassion brings. 'He will beautify the meek with salvation' is the word of God. The life which comes to know the love of God in Christ can and will be made lovely again.

Power

You shall receive power, after that the Holy Ghost is come upon
you . . .
ACTS 1:8

THE promise given by Christ before Pentecost
was that with the coming of the Holy Spirit the
church would receive 'power'. . .'Ye shall
receive power after that the Holy Ghost is come upon
you.' If that promise is true (and can it be otherwise?),
then there is nothing so urgent or so relevant to the
need of the church today as a study of the Person and
work of the Holy Spirit, set out in the Word of God.

A study of the chapter which describes the events
of that first Whit Sunday as recorded in Acts 2, will
give us some clues as to the nature of this transforming
power that is available in the Holy Spirit.

It meant **power to stand.** In verse 14 we read of
Peter 'standing up'. Think of *the fear that had crippled
them*. Yes, he was able to stand now whereas before he
had run away! Is there anything more needed today
than the ability on the part of the Christian to stand?
The flood of evil and apathy is running at full tide and
it is so easy to drift with it, to give way to it.

This is just what the church has been doing and
what so many Christians are doing still. Giving way,
yielding, surrendering when they ought to be standing
up and standing firm.

Is this the picture and image of most Christians
today? Think of *the fact that had changed them*. There is
a desperate need for some who will be willing to stand
rock-like in the midst of the turbulent currents of our
modern times. Will you be one of these? If you will,

then you will need the power of the Holy Spirit in your life.

It meant **power to speak.** There was *no hint of apology*. We read in that same verse of Peter not simply standing up, but of him speaking up. He 'lifted up his voice' and somehow I don't think he spoke in a whisper or with a note of apology in his voice. Peter's was a voice that had had to rise above the sound of wind and storm and wave on the Sea of Galilee. It would be a powerful voice and it would echo and re-echo down the streets nearby!

There was the *clear note of authority*. The Holy Spirit gave Peter power to speak, and this is desperately needed today. We need ordinary folk who will speak up and speak out for righteousness and truth, for Christ and the church, in your office, among your friends or among the family. Power to speak, how much we need this!

It meant also **power to see;** the ability to *understand the mind of God* and the truth of God. Before Pentecost Peter and the others were all wrong in their thinking about the purpose of God in Christ, even in Acts 1 we read of them still thinking of a political kingdom and not a spiritual one.

But after Pentecost his understanding was complete. We need laymen today who understand the nature and relevance of the Christian faith. And this is just what the Holy Spirit can do, 'When he the spirit of truth is come, he will guide you into all truth.'

Ask God to help you to know the transforming power of the Holy Spirit in your own life, and have the ability to *undertake the work of God*, that work which takes the message of God's saving grace to the uttermost parts of the earth!

. . . *Like a Garden*

Thou shalt be like a watered garden
ISAIAH 58:11

T HESE words are found in Isaiah 58:11 and are most suggestive. There are all kinds of gardens. They are found everywhere. On the roofs of big stores, on the window-boxes of soaring tenements, tucked away in unexpected and unlikely backyards, or out in the more spacious countryside. They are in every conceivable kind of condition, some beautifully and lovingly cared for, others neglected and derelict. So it is with life.

There is work in a garden. If a garden is to be beautiful and fruitful, it will always be the result of work! Some folk seem to think that they can laze their way to excellence of character, to depth of spiritual worth.

There will be always work *by a person*. In a garden there will always be the evidence of the work of the hands of someone, their footprints will be seen, the results of their designing and planning. Lovely gardens don't just happen. They are the result of work. So with lovely lives. And what gardener is better fitted to undertake this work in the garden of the soul than the unseen but living Lord of life, Jesus Christ.

There will always be work *at a price!* There will be cost in terms of money, of labour, of strength. In industry working hours are getting shorter and shorter. But there is never any off-time in the work of living. We find it demanding and exhausting. There is always a price to be paid.

There are weeds in a garden. No garden, however beautiful, is free from the perils of weeds. Gardens have only to be left for a while and the weeds

48   *Top*—Boyish adventure
                                       Bottom—Happy Christianity ▶

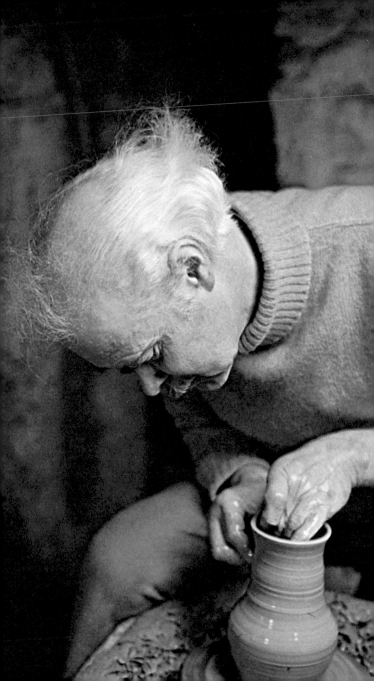

will soon manifest themselves. So the life that is neglectful of the means of grace will swiftly revert to its old state.

Think *how weeds spoil*. They suffocate by their strength and growth that which is intended to bloom and flower. They sting if they are nettles. They stab if they are thistles. Our Lord spoke of thorns choking the good seed. Weeds do that.

Think *how weeds spread*. Let some weeds into your garden and they will spread until there is not a part of the garden where they cannot be found. So with the unworthy things in life, the unattractive, the sins and the failures. They have a strength that seems to affect every part of life.

There is wealth in a garden. There is a potential of beauty, of fragrance, of flower, of fruit, waiting to be produced.

These will bring *enjoyment to many*. What a pleasure some gardens give to others; some lives give to others.

These will mean *enrichment for others*, for from the produce of the garden, others will go away laden down with what they have received. So some lives are indeed 'like a garden'. The question we each have to ask is, quite simply, are our lives like one? Is yours?

Clearing the Old Wells

Isaac digged again the wells of water, which they had digged in the days of Abraham his father

GENESIS 26:18, 19

THE well is used more than once in the Bible to illustrate the grace of God in man's experience. See, for instance, Isaiah 12:13 and John 4:14. Just as to the tribesman the well meant the difference between poverty and prosperity, death and life, so is the experience of God's grace to the Christian.

There is **a truth** in these verses: every generation must discover God's grace for itself. Isaac had to dig just as his father had before him, but in doing so, he had the memory that lingered!

The names of the wells were remembered! 'He called their names after the names by which his father had called them.' Isaac remembered not only where the wells were to be found, but their names. How many of us have memories of the wells at which our fathers drank, memories of family prayers and Bible readings, and find in them inspiration and help in our Christian living.

The need for the wells was accepted! These wells were essential to the lives of our fathers, the centre of their spiritual inspiration. That quietly spent Sunday set apart for God was one such well. The Bible, well worn, well thumbed and well read, was the instrument through which God's voice came to them. The Cross of our Lord, about which so many of the hymns they loved were written, was the centre of their hope.

If there is truth here, there is **tragedy** also. The wells had been stopped up, 'the Philistines had stopped them.' That suggests *the presence of an enemy*. The Bible makes abundantly clear the existence of the forces of

50

evil, a trinity of the world with its allurements, the flesh with its subtlety, the devil with his experiences. Whenever I hear people denying the existence of the devil, I want to reply like the schoolboy, 'If there is no devil, then who is doing all his dirty work?'

The Bible speaks of 'your adversary, the devil'. *The purpose of the enemy* is to destroy those they bitterly resent. They attacked the wells knowing that if they were stopped up, life itself became impossible.

In our lives, too, the purpose of the enemy is to destroy, and he will attack the wells. The Bible is unread, the church not entered, the Sunday mispent, the Cross forgotten, the soul starved, the life impoverished. We read the newspaper, we have been in bed, or in the car instead of going to church. The Sunday that used to be given to God is spent on ourselves.

But there is also **a task.** 'And Isaac digged again . . .' To clear the wells meant hard work, the soil had to be removed, see how *the enemy was fought* and resisted, but note *the discovery that was made*. 'They digged . . . and found there a well of springing water.' What a thrilling moment when Isaac digged and springs gushed up, sparkling and cool. The same discovery can be ours. The wells our fathers digged held living water. They were not just the habits of a formal religion. If we dig in the same wells we too will find springing water.

Isaac knew where to find the wells because his father had digged them. Do our children know where to find the wells? The day will come when they discover their need of living water. Do they know the way to the wells so that they will know where to turn, because of the legacy we have left them?

Sword Drill

The sword of the Spirit

EPHESIANS 6:17

THE young man taking the Children's Service on the beach soon let us know what he meant. He was referring to the Bible, called by Paul, 'the sword of the Spirit', and as the children drew their Bibles and New Testaments from their pockets and raised them on high, they sang the chorus 'Draw your swords, use your swords, for the battle is the Lord's'.

It set me thinking of 'Sword Drill'.

I thought of **the practice with the sword.** We all realise the *importance* of practice in almost everything. I heard of a pianist who said, 'If I miss my seven hours practice for one day I know it, if I miss it for two days the critics know it, if I miss it for three days the public knows it.'

Standing in a proud position in our lounge is a Cricket Cup won by my son, largely I think because of the practice that we had together in the garden. How important it is that we should be familiar with our Bibles, because we all realise the *difference* that practice makes, the difference between success and failure, between defeat and victory. So often the child who fails is the one who hasn't practised.

The second thought that came to me concerned **the place for the sword.** In Nehemiah 4:18 we read 'Everyone had his sword girded by his side.' If the Bible is 'the sword of the Spirit' then we want to have it available. There are two places where we should keep the Bible, the first, *in our hearts*. The psalmist puts it 'Thy word have I hid in my heart that I might not sin against thee.' There is a tremendous value in learning verses of the Bible by heart; in being so familiar with passages that we almost know them by heart.

But we also must keep the Bible *in our hands*. We ought to have a Bible handy enough to carry around with us, small enough to go into our jacket pocket, or small enough to slip into our handbag. We never know when we might need it and the place for the Bible is not a forgotten place in a drawer of a bookcase, but in the place where we can get at it quickly.

The last thought that came to my mind concerned **the power in the sword,** and here of course the sword of the Spirit, which is the Word of God, is so different from the sword used on the battlefield. It is the power first of all *to create life*. In 1 Peter 1:23 we read of those who were 'born again by the Word of God'.

One of the strange facts about the Bible is that it can do just that very thing and create new life within the soul. But for the Christian it is the power also *to protect life*. I wonder if you have read the story of the Pilgrim's Progress and if so whether you recollect how Christian came down into the Valley of Humiliation where Apollyon met him and gave him a dreadful fall. In that fall his sword flew out of his hand and Apollyon cried out 'I am sure of thee now!'

Even the devil realises that the Christian is defenceless apart from his Bible, but you remember how Christian stretched his hand for his sword and caught it again and gave Apollyon a deadly thrust.

Yes, I learnt a lesson from those children singing their chorus so happily on the beach! The importance of sword drill. I wonder whether you treat your Bible as something you simply dare not live without?

Love's Refusal

Neither will I offer . . . that which doth cost me nothing

2 SAMUEL 24:24

WE might do well to think out together something of the costliness that marks all true love and devotion.

In this connection there are some challenging words which are to be found in 2 Samuel 24:24, when David speaks, 'Neither will I offer unto the Lord my God of that which doth cost me nothing.' An easy and cheap devotion had been offered to David, but the love in David's heart rose in revolt against such a thought.

Let us think out the meaning of his words, and let us think of ourselves giving ourselves in love and devotion to our God. 'Neither will I offer unto the Lord my God of that which doth cost me nothing.'

The claim that love makes. David speaks here about 'the Lord *my* God'. There is something very *possessive* about love, something intimately personal. David does not speak about the Lord, but about the Lord *my* God! Even in human relationship that same note is struck. A mother speaks of 'my child', the child of 'my kitten'. One friend speaks of another as 'my friend' and a husband speaks of 'my wife'.

That personal possessiveness of love suggests that love's offering must be *personal* too. The thought that was intolerable to David was that he should offer to God something that was not his own, 'that which doth cost *me* nothing'. How many folk, alas, know little of this personal relationship, this personal devotion.

The constraint that love knows. David is here occupied with the thought of what he can *give*, of what he can offer to the Lord—with giving, not getting! If there is in true love an element of possessiveness, there is also an element of utter unselfishness, of a *desire* to give to the one loved. In these modern days of increasing moral laxity how many of our young folk go wrong in their conception of what love is. The physical and emotional stimulus that such laxity indulges in is mistaken for love, while all the time at its heart is a selfish and sinful pleasure in what is received rather than a joy in what is given.

What a constant giving marks a mother's love for her child; a giving of her very self at the beginning, a giving at any time of day or night, a giving whether tired or not, a giving whether thanked or not, a giving almost to the end of her days, for no child ever outgrows the need for the mother's hand and the mother's voice. And, what *delight* too marks the giving of love!

This 'giving' of love marks the love of God, who 'so loved the world that he gave'. But in our spiritual experience where is the emphasis, is it on giving or getting? In our life in the fellowship of Christ's church, are we concerned to give or get? How glorious are the givers, how grumbly are the getters.

The costliness that love demands. It was the cheapness of the way offered to him that revolted the mind of David. To offer to the Lord his God that which cost him nothing was utterly abhorrent to him. Love is *not only willing to pay a price,* but love *insists that there should be a price to pay.*

How many of us have known what it is to buy a present for someone we loved, and when we went to the shop we found ourselves looking for the gift not among the cheap things that we could easily afford, but among the expensive things we knew we ought not really to purchase.

Do you not feel that the Christian church needs today to rediscover this mark of real and true devotion to her Lord? So much of our church and Christian work is determined by our convenience or comfort. If the weather is decent we go. If we have nothing more important to do we will turn up.

And when it comes to giving money, well, we give

55

to God and his church what we would give for a tip, and far less than a man would give for a packet of cigarettes, and then we think we have done our bit, while all the time the truth of the matter is that we have given to the Lord our God that which has cost us nothing.

The choice that love exercises. Human love is *selective*, we choose when, what, and whom we are going to love, and upon them we lavish our thoughts and affections. The thought in my own mind is that we should offer a more costly devotion to *Christ*. How many Christians there are who give and spend lavishly upon themselves, upon some hobby or sport. Love is also *decisive!*

Why not give a costly devotion to Christ your Lord, taking the words of David the king, 'neither will I offer unto the Lord my God that which doth cost me nothing', and making them your own?

A Famous Walk

Jesus himself drew near, and went with them

LUKE 24:15

OF the many stories about the risen Saviour, possibly the choicest is that recorded in Luke 24, the walk to Emmaus.

The two disciples deep in conversation realised suddenly that a stranger had joined them. They discussed the strange events of the past days, the shattering of all their hopes. The stranger seemed, however, to throw a new light altogether on the conversation, and showed them that the events leading up to the death of Christ were part of God's eternal purpose. As he spoke their hearts burned within them, and reaching their destination they asked him to 'Abide with us'. He went in, and as they sat at their simple meal, he gave thanks, breaking the bread. In that moment they knew him. It was Christ himself. No wonder they hastened back to tell the other disciples the amazing, unbelievable news, that Christ was risen.

In this simple story of a walk along a country road and its ending, we can see some lessons to help us in our journey through life. Think of **the presence that touched their lives** *Unrecognised* by the disciples 'Jesus himself drew near, and went with them'. They were aware of his presence, although they did not know him, and their hearts were so moved as he spoke to them, that later they said 'Did not our hearts burn within us?' So comforing and strengthening was his presence that when they reached their journey's end they asked him to remain with them. Not knowing who he was, not quite understanding what it all meant, they did not want the experience to end. And so, the living Christ still draws near to our hearts today, and still he is long unrecognised, but to thinking minds and troubled hearts his presence not only brings peace but creates a desire for its continuance.

But the presence that was unrecognised at first was later *unmistakable*. We read in verse 30 'their eyes were opened and they knew him', in the breaking of bread. How they recognised him we are not told. It may have been the scar on the hands that broke the bread, but they knew that he was the Christ. It was a brief moment of recognition, for we read 'Immediately he vanished out of their sight'.

That moment of recognition still comes to the hearts of men, when suddenly we know the reality of Jesus Christ as the living Saviour.

Now notice **the problems that troubled their minds.** As we watch these men walking along the road we feel *their disappointment*: 'We trusted that . . .' Men and women still face such disappointments and frustrations. Life and its pleasure does not satisfy them. We are also struck by *the disciples' evident distress*. In verse 17, Christ sees they are sad. Their grief was so bitter they could not stop talking or thinking about it.

How many have lost the secret of real happiness. It was to two such men that the presence of the living Christ came with help and healing in his voice. The final point of comparison lies in **the purpose that transformed their future.** After Christ had made himself known to them they were transformed. Whatever their programme had been, it was thrown topsy-turvy in the thrill of their discovery. Christ can still bring momentary confusion into our lives and well-ordered plans. What he has to say, what he himself is; these are such tremendous truths, that once they really grip a man's heart they are the things that matter most. They learned of *a purpose that was exciting*.

Look at verse 27, 'Beginning at Moses . . .' These men suddenly realised that in Christ they were touching something which reached back in history and stretched forward into the future. The whole meaning of history suddenly broke upon their souls.

Life would, henceforth, be without meaning apart

from this relationship to God. But this *purpose was also exacting*. Hurrying back to Jerusalem they met the others who in due time received the great commission from Christ himself, 'As my Father has sent me, even so I sent you'. What a wonderful purpose and privilege, and it all started when one day on a country walk Christ drew near and went with them, and as he talked, suddenly they knew 'him'.

Do We Keep Our Promises?

When thou vowest a vow
ECCLESIASTES 5:4

THERE is a short passage in the book of Ecclesiastes concerning the vows we make to God. Turn it up and read the words over thoughtfully. You will find them in the fifth chapter and in the first seven verses. Here are some thoughts that I would like to share with you.

We have here first of all **God's plea for restraint** (vv. 1 and 2). 'When thou goest to the house of God be not rash with thy mouth to utter anything before God.' One of the characteristics of the ministry of Christ was the restraint he was always imposing upon would-be disciples. *What are the reasons for such restraint?* Sometimes the reason may have to do with the circumstances under which vows are made.

So often we vow to God when we are in trouble (Psalm 66:13, 14). But troubles can pass. Sometimes a man will vow to God under the stress of some great emotion, like Jacob did at Bethel. But emotions can subside. The trouble with such vows is that so often they do not involve the whole man.

What are the results of such restraint? The results can be seen in the quality of discipleship secured. Christ picked only twelve men, but look at the work they did. Today the church has hundreds and thousands, but how little is achieved.

We have also in these verses what I have called **God's preference for refusal.** 'Better it is that thou shouldest not vow than that thou shouldest vow and not pay.' There is the twofold thought here, first of *the tragedy that God would avert*, 'that thou shouldest not vow'. What greater tragedy can there be in the spiritual experience of a man or woman than that their life should be one marked by no response whatever to the voice and will of God. That the opportunities given by God should have been lost, that the striving of God the Holy Spirit should have all been in vain, that the vision given should have been forgotten, the circumstances created at such infinite pains by God should all have proved of no avail.

'That thou shouldest not vow', is a tragedy of the greatest magnitude that God will do everything to avert. But there is another thought and it is of this that these words speak, the thought of *the travesty that God would avoid*. 'Better it is that thou shouldest not vow than that thou shouldest vow and not pay.' The travesty of Christianity that God will do anything to avoid is that of lip religion, that experience which contents itself with words and not deeds. Christianity is not a matter of pious talk, or correct vocabulary, it is the experience and expression of the life of Christ revealed in and through human personality. Who was it who wrote those words, 'To call Jesus Lord is orthodoxy, to call him Lord, Lord, is piety; but to call him Lord, Lord and do not the things which he commands is blasphemy'?

The last thought that I find in these verses is what I have called **God's passion for reality.** 'When thou vowest a vow . . . defer not to pay it.' I note here two things. First, *there is an assumption that God makes*, 'When thou vowest' God does not say, 'if', but 'when'. The assumption is that all of us at one time or another do make a vow to God. Is that true of you as you read these words?

What an unfolding of human experience we would have, what a story of God's dealing with men, if we could take any congregation of Christian people, and have told us the story of the vows they have made to God. We would hear of confirmations, of dark hours of bereavement, of some great convention meeting, of the birth of many children, of marriage services, of hours of danger.

We would be taken into many hospital wards and nursing homes, the walls of many rooms would be called to bear their witness; the voices of a thousand preachers would sound in our ears, we would be taken to almost every page of the Word of God. Yes, the vows have been made, and God is right in making such an assumption.

But look, there is one more thought here. There is the thought of *the action God wants*: 'when thou vowest . . . defer not to pay it.' Here is the thought of a postponement that has been allowed and God says 'defer not'. Yes, the vow has been made but the payment of it has been deferred. We do well to remember that delayed obedience is disobedience. When did you make your vow to God? and how long have you been putting off the payment of it?

Yes, a postponement has been allowed and a payment must be made. 'Pay that which thou hast vowed.' How personal that vow was, your own lips framed the words and uttered them, it concerned something about which no one else knew anything at all. It was your vow, God expects you to be faithful. What was that vow? Go now and pay it.

The Lord's Day

The sabbath was made for man

MARK 2.27

I QUESTION if there is anything less properly understood than the Sabbath Day, or the Lord's Day, as the Christian will call it.

The best known verses about it are often the least accurately, or least fully, quoted. They come in Mark 2:27, 28 'The sabbath was made for man and not man for the sabbath; therefore the Son of man is Lord also of the sabbath.'

Have you noticed how, when these words are quoted, the last sentence is almost always left out, 'therefore the Son of man is Lord also of the sabbath'?

But let us look at these words a little more closely and see what they reveal.

In the first place we can see **the love that planned for it.** 'The sabbath was made for man,' says Christ, made, conceived by the love of God. Let us think for a moment of *the intention of divine love*. So often the attitude of men's minds is that the sabbath is meant to be a dreary and dull day, but does love ever intend to make life like that? Surely the complete opposite is the case.

Love always seeks to enrich and never to impoverish. And let us think also of *the insight of divine love*. Love knows best what is the need of the one loved. Others may make mistakes but love's insight tells it where the need lies. Let us never forget then that the whole idea of one day's rest in seven was born out of the love in the heart of God for man.

In the second place we can think of **the life that will profit by it.** Our Lord says that 'the sabbath was made for man'. It was made for *the whole of man*. And let us never forget that this includes the soul. Man's body and mind need to be rested and man's soul needs to be fed and nourished. It was with this in view that the day of rest, the day to be set apart in a special way for God, was designed.

It was made not only for the whole of man but also for *the good of man*. It was 'made for man', the sabbath was made for man's good. Man needs one day in seven when the pace slows down and there is rest. Man will be all the better, all the fitter for the sabbath and all the worse for neglecting it or destroying it. How true the old saying 'A sabbath well spent brings a week of content'.

In the last place we can think of **the lord that must preside over it.** 'The Son of man is Lord also of the sabbath day.' In a very special sense his authority must be acknowledged on this day. I will be able to spend *more time with him* in the worship of the church and in the fellowship of his people. I will give *more thought to him*. So often during the week my thoughts are busy with other important and necessary things and people, but on this day, I can turn from them and turn to think of him.

'This is the day the Lord hath made, let us rejoice and be glad in it.'

Top—The city lights of Chicago
Bottom—The Golden Pagoda, Kyoto, Japan ▶

Recipe for Living

Seek ye first the kingdom of God

MATTHEW 6:33

WE may or may not have heard the story of the American who had embroidered on his tie the letters B.A.I.K. When asked what they meant, he replied that they stood for 'Boy, Am I Konfused'—when his questioner replied 'But you don't spell "confused" with a "K",' he retorted, 'Boy, you don't know how "Confused" I am!'

Into the confusion that prevails today everywhere and all the time, the words of Jesus Christ come with both an atmosphere of sanity and of serenity—the words that I call 'a recipe for living'. Here they are: 'Seek ye first the kingdom of God and his righteousness, and all these things will be added unto you.'

The recipe includes three ingredients—I will name them, I want you to try them:

The presence of the king: these words speak of a kingdom—but you cannot have a kingdom without a king. For us in relationship to Jesus Christ this involves us in two things:

There must be an acceptance of the person on the throne—there must be an acceptance of the person of Christ into my life and yours—this and no less than this is involved here. 'He that hath the Son hath the life.' You cannot be a Christian, without having Christ!

There must be an allegiance to the Power of the Throne—the right of this Man to rule must be accepted. Jesus Christ is not only Saviour but Sovereign too. I must obey my Sovereign as well as accept my Saviour.

The priority of the king: these words speak of seeking '*first* the kingdom of God'. It is not enough to

The cable car at Chateau d'Oex, Switzerland

E

have the right ingredients, I must follow the right order.

There are the rivals that would seduce my allegiance: 'the world, the flesh and the devil' will all clamour for my prior consideration. I will court disaster if I heed them.

There is the resolve that will secure my obedience: 'First' is the only place for my Lord. I will then seek diligently to find out what his wishes are and as diligently seek to meet them before heeding any other voice.

The promise of the king: '. . . and all these things will be added unto you.'

We do well to remember:

The responsibility of a king—it is his to secure the well-being of the subjects over whose lives he exercises his rule.

The resources of a king—if this king be the Creator God, these resources on which he will draw are limitless.

To have been translated from the kingdom of darkness to that of light is to be translated from confusion to order and peace.

A Beautiful Church

How lovely is thy dwelling-place

PSALM 84:1 (metrical version)

EVERY summer many people explore the beauties of the countryside and no doubt visit the lovely churches that are found everywhere. It was not yesterday that someone wrote 'How lovely is thy dwelling place, O Lord of hosts, to me'. What lies behind the loveliness that you and the psalmist both see?

There may be **the beauty of adornment.** The church may be beautiful because of *the lovely things found there*. The furnishings, the design of the building, the flowers so tastefully arranged by loving hands, all these may be lovely. How right that they should be!

There is a rare beauty in God's natural creation, of form and of colour, which reflects surely, in part, the beauty that must be inherent in the divine nature. As a home will reflect the characters of those who live in it, so the house of God should reflect, however inadequately, the character of God.

The beauty that adorns may lie in *the lovely lives lived there*. 1 Peter 3:3, speaks of 'a hidden adorning' that is in the sight of God of great price. And in spite of much failure the story of every church has seldom lacked this kind of beauty; lovely lives lived within its fellowship, drawing their loveliness from the grace of God which they have found there.

There may be also **the beauty of association.** How lovely certain places will always be to us because of the lovely things that happened there.

The beauty of association may be that of *contentment* and of happiness. How things and places are touched into beauty by the content and happiness that

67

filled our hearts when we were there. The loveliest home that husband and wife ever know is usually the first, just because it is viewed through that glow of happiness that was so newly and wonderfully theirs.

How lovely are the places in which we spent the holidays of our childhood. Go back to them now and to other eyes they may seem ordinary but never to ours. Has the church not this same association, what happiness is there after all to compare with that which the psalmist calls 'the joy of our salvation'. What church can ever be anything but lovely if in that church we found that joy!

But there is also the association of *achievement*. Sometimes a day has been in a special sense a 'lovely day' and we trace this to a deeper level. The day has been so worthwhile, help has been given or received, service or success have been rendered! Keswick is a lovely place in the heart of the English Lake District, but to thousands of Christians its beauty is the beauty of association, for there, as almost nowhere else, have the days spent at the great Christian convention been days worthwhile, when help has been given or received.

We cannot omit **the beauty of affection.** There is in life a *loveliness that love alone sees*. To every child granted a mother's love, that mother's face will always be lovely. And where does love touch our lives so richly as in the church, its worship and fellowship, when we see and sense the love of God in the face of Jesus Christ.

And that means that there will be *a faithfulness that love always shows*. For as we grow older honesty may compel us to admit that there are flaws in the beauty even of a mother's face, but flaws or not, our love and loyalty live on.

The church has her faults too and her blemishes, but if in her life and love we have found the love of life of God in Christ, the words of the psalmist will always be the words of our testimony:

'How lovely is thy dwelling place,
  O Lord of hosts, to me.'

Come as the Fire

The spirit of burning
ISAIAH 4:4

T HERE is possibly no greater need in the church than a rediscovery of the purpose and ministry of the Holy Spirit as the 'Spirit of burning' (Isaiah 4:4).

In Scotland, when a movement of the Spirit of God begins in the Highlands and Islands they speak of 'Fire among the Heather'.

As the Spirit of burning he can **burn through men's defences.** Fire has always been a weapon of war, from the fire-tipped arrows of the Red Indians to the flame throwers of modern war strategy. Fire destroys, disintegrates and disorganises the defence of an enemy against attack.

Think of *the barriers that protect men engaged in battle.* Men erect them in an attempt to hide from the challenge of the divine intention. The last thing that man is prepared to do is to surrender his will to the will of his Creator. This citadel he will defend to the death. Intellectual difficulties, physical distance, moral decency, rational dishonesty, he will erect these and other barriers and is determined to defend them to the bitter end. His position seems invincible!

But consider also *the burning that penetrates.* It is the penetration of such barriers that is the precise work of the Holy Spirit. Our Lord promised concerning him, 'When he is come he will convict the world of sin and of righteousness and of judgment.' The Holy Spirit can achieve a penetration that no human cleverness can ever achieve. How desperately we need to see this penetration in these days.

69

As the Spirit of burning he can **burn out sin's dross.** This conception of the purifying ministry of fire is familiar in the word of God. In Isaiah 1:25: 'I will purge away thy dross'; in Malachi 3:3: 'He shall sit as a refiner and purifier of silver.'

What *a revealing process* this will be. The moment the Holy Spirit becomes not only resident but operative in the heart and life of a man, the revealing process begins. We find to our amazement that while we thought we were pretty good types before we were converted, now we seem to develop a sensitivity of conscience that is almost an embarrassment. Perfection is the new standard and the Holy Spirit is content with nothing less.

But what *a resultant purity* there will be. In Isaiah 1:25 the purging is to produce pureness; in Malachi 3:3 it is in order 'that they may offer unto the Lord an offering in righteousness'. The standard is high but the reason is sound. Man has been made for God and therefore for righteousness and man can never find happiness until he fulfils his destiny.

Finally, as the Spirit of burning he can **burn in God's design.** How *lovely* that design is. Everyone who has visited a pottery will have seen this attribute of fire. The way it burns in the colour and beauty is fascinating to watch.

But the colours painted on by the artist seem to bear little likeness to the colours which emerge from the heat. So it is with the disciplines and providences that the Holy Spirit uses in his dealings with us.

But there is also the permanency of the work. The fire produces results which are not only lovely but also *lasting*. If the colours had been merely painted on they would in due time come off. It is the fire that burns them in. The work of the Spirit of burning is designed to last for time and for eternity.

Come thou burning Spirit, come.

No Substitute

The word of God, which liveth and abideth
1 PETER 1:23

'BEING born again not of corruptible seed but of incorruptible, by the word of God which liveth and abideth for ever.' So writes Peter in his first epistle, and his words suggest three thoughts about the 'word of God' which we might well remember.

The first relates to **the time it endures.** He speaks of it as an 'incorruptible' seed, of a word which 'liveth and abideth for ever'. *How transient* are so many of the influences in our lives. We can think of the influence of a friendship. Most of us have known what it is to find at one time or other in our lives that we have come to owe more than we have been able to tell to the help that has been ours through friendship with another Christian, possibly more deeply taught in the things of the Spirit than ourselves, but then circumstances separated us from that one.

Or it may have been that we have owed a tremendous debt to the ministry of a certain church, until we left the church or there was a change of minister. It may have been that we owed a great deal to our home, until we lost our parents or left the home. These things all played their part, but the sadness of them all was that they did not 'abide for ever'.

How different the ministry of the Word. How vital that in every Christian this abiding ministry should be exercised. How comforting to the worker to know that the seed of the Word which he has been enabled to plant is an incorruptible seed, that it will indeed endure and abide for ever. How blessed to the one who has been ministered to by others to know that the same wealth, indeed a far greater wealth of ministry, can be found in the Word. The time it endures, this alone makes the Bible indispensable in spiritual experience.

The second point to note relates to **the task it effects.** 'Born again . . . by the word.' The Word of God plays an *indispensable* part in the work of regeneration. The result of its work might not be seen immediately. It might lie dormant in the heart and mind of the hearer for many years. But the seed was 'incorruptible'. And this seed would be the instrument in the hand of God for the creation of the new life within the soul.

How *essential* that in our sermons, in our Sunday School lessons, we should be sowing the seed. Not content with the achieving of a reputation for popularity or cleverness, not content simply that we have held the attention of the children with interesting stories, but that we should know that we have sowed the seed of the Word of God in the mind of the hearers.

Is this the reason why a good deal of the preaching of today lacks in spiritual result, because men and teachers have felt it more important to proclaim what they think rather than what God has said? If we want to witness the birth of new life it is absolutely essential that the 'incorruptible seed' should be planted in the hearts and minds of those to whom we minister. Here again the Bible is absolutely indispensable.

The third thought relates to **the trust it evokes.** We need never lack *confidence* in the proclamation of our message as long as it is the 'Word of God'. If it was a message of our own contriving, we might well hesitate. If our work was dependent upon the duration of our own immediate influence upon those to whom we minister we might indeed tremble for their spiritual well-being. But this word, this 'incorruptible seed' which we are called to sow, divine in its origin, its authority and its power, inspires in our hearts a confidence and trust that nothing else could, and gives *permanence* to our work.

Today there is a need for a note of authority in our preaching. That note of authority, that sense of confidence, will come not from our eloquence, not from our erudition, but from the fact that the message we proclaim is not the word of man, but the word of God.

Unanswered Prayer

Ye have not, because ye ask not

JAMES 4:2

LET us look at this problem a little more closely. Why are so many prayers unanswered?

The first reason I would give is that **the practice of prayer has been discontinued.** Part of the problem of unanswered prayer is that of unoffered prayer! Cf. James 4:2 'Ye have not because ye ask not.'

The practice of prayer has been discontinued *in the life of the Christian.* 'When thou prayest,' said Jesus Christ, 'enter into thy room and when thou hast shut thy door, pray.' But how seldom is this done today even by converted, professing Christian people.

The practice of prayer has been discontinued *in the life of the church.* In Acts 12:12 we read that 'many were gathered together praying'. When revival broke out in Dundee in the church of Robert Murray McCheyne he reported that there were thirty-nine meetings for prayer being held every week!

And yet today prayer-meetings are so out of fashion that few churches have them, and where a church has one, so few people come, and even they scarcely ever pray.

The second reason I would give is that **the person who prays has been disqualified.** We do well to stop and ask ourselves as individuals what right we have to expect God to answer our prayers. There are at least two reasons why a person might expect to be disqualified.

Somebody may be disqualified because *a relationship has never been established* with God, not a right relationship. We cannot expect God to answer our prayers unless he is our Father, and he is not our

Father unless we are his born-again children cf. John 1:12.

Somebody may also be disqualified because *a rebellion has never been ended*. 'If I regard iniquity in my heart the Lord will not hear me' (Psalm 66:18). If there is rebellion then the motive in my prayer is sure to be wrong and 'Ye ask, and receive not, because ye ask amiss' (James 4:3).

The third reason I would suggest is that **the petition in the prayer has been denied.** Let us be prepared for God to say 'no' and let us remember that 'no' is just as much an answer as 'yes'.

God may say 'no' because of *the harm it would do* if he said 'yes'. Every parent has to say 'no' to a child who does not understand what the request involves.

The petition may be denied because of *the test this can be*, for what God is saying is not 'no' but 'wait'. And in that waiting he wants to see how far we are prepared to trust his love and wisdom.

Is a Man a Sheep?

All we like sheep have gone astray

ISAIAH 53:6

SOME time ago I read an article in one of our national weekly papers in which a journalist wrote in a somewhat scathing manner about the standard of preaching in the pulpits of our land today. I felt that in all probability a great deal of his criticism was justified. On one point however I would have crossed swords with him. He complained bitterly that in several of the services he attended the preacher spoke of Christ as the Good Shepherd and mankind as the sheep. It seemed to him to be futile and irrelevant to preach such a message in our modern space age.

My mind went instinctively to the twenty-third psalm, the shepherd psalm of the Old Testament, and I thought of its immense popularity and suitability at almost every occasion, from a christening or a wedding, to a funeral. My mind leapt quickly to the parable of the lost sheep and back to that prophetic utterance 'all we *like sheep* have gone astray, we have turned everyone to his own way'.

I felt the conviction growing within me that the journalist was wrong and the Scriptures were right. Men are like sheep and the sooner they own up to the fact the better for themselves and for everyone else. Turn and read the opening verses of Luke 15, the parable of the lost sheep, and then ponder these thoughts.

There are three statements that come instinctively to mind as we read the story and imagine the scene and then as we look at life as we see it around us.

The sheep was foolish as men are foolish; and that in two ways. Foolish in what it believed and in how it behaved. *In what it believed*. The sheep presumably thought that it knew better than the shepherd. Did the shepherd warn of dangers and perils in the wilderness? Did he light fires at night to frighten away the wild creatures of the night? Did he sleep, ever watchful, across the entrance to the fold?

Had not experience warned the flock a hundred times of their inability to cope with their foes? But the sheep either forgot or thought otherwise, if it thought at all, as so many men so seldom think. Yes, the sheep knew better than the shepherd and could manage well without his supervision.

Not only was the sheep foolish in what it believed but also *in how it behaved*. I wonder how often this sheep had tried to get away on its own, to be brought back by the shepherd's watchful care. How often had the shepherd warned it, spoken to it. It is so with men. We are stubborn creatures as well as foolish, and the warnings of God are as frequent as our foolish attempts to break free from his care and his will.

The sheep was frightened as men are frightened. It might have been fun at first with the sun shining; it was in a new, big and exciting world. But when night came it was different.

Two new factors entered into its experience, neither of them pleasant. It discovered that *it was lonely*. Not that there were not other living creatures, but they were not interested in a sheep! The shadows grew longer, the sun sunk lower, the sky became darker. How lonely life can become for men. How little and insignificant we can find ourselves to be in a big city in this large world. How little others care what happens to us. Everyone is looking after himself.

It discovered *it was lost*. It wanted no doubt to get back to the flock and to the shepherd, but it just did not know how to find the way. And as it made its frightened way in the darkness it got hurt. Men today are all questing for something more adequate for the demands of life than their own resources, and they just can't find the answer they seek.

The sheep was found as men are found. That

lost sheep was missed by one person, the shepherd as he counted his flock that night! Men who have turned their backs upon God's love are missed too.

Think as we close *how hurt love is* when it finds that it has not been trusted, but the shepherd's hurt was more than a hurt in the heart, his hands and feet were wounded too as he searched for the sheep that was lost. Have not both the heart and hands of Christ the marks of the wounds of our inflicting? *How happy love is* when the sheep is found and safe again. The shepherd and the sheep are together again and both are happy again!

Have You Done as Much?

She hath done what she could

MARK 14:8

ONE of the choicest incidents in the life of our Lord is found among the gathering shadows as he approached the cross. It is recorded in Mark 14:1–19; John 12.

Note **the service rendered.** It is a woman who renders this service and John describes the ointment that was poured out as 'very costly'. Mark describes it as 'very precious'. In view of its value of three hundred pence, it was *an extravagant offering.* The word extravagant means a going beyond what could be expected, beyond what would be reasonable.

How much, or how little of the service we render to Christ today can be thus described . . . 'very costly'? We live in a day when the legitimate in service is carefully defined. The trade unions see to that. No doubt such exactitude is a necessary thing to protect the workers. But is there not a danger of exactness becoming the pattern of every relationship and every responsibility? 'I'm not paid to do that', means so often that the thing is left undone.

Consider also how it was *a fragrant offering.* John tells us that 'the house was filled with the odour of the ointment'. What are the most fragrant memories in most folk's lives? Surely they are the memories of childhood, because then most of us knew the most unselfish ministry of love that we shall ever know, the care of a mother's love. How unstinted, unbargaining, is such a love and because of this a fragrance clings to those wonderful days.

Note **the standards reached.** 'She hath done *what she could*' was the Master's tribute. *There was a thoroughness in what she did.* There were certain things she could not do, and which Christ would never have expected of her. But what she could do she did, and did it up to the utmost limit. How few of us are fit to stand beside this simple woman of long ago!

There was thoughtfulness in what she did. 'She is come aforehand to anoint my body to the burying.' Only Mary was in tune with the mood and mind of the Saviour that day. Love made her sensitive and she knew that the shadow of the cross was dark across his heart, and she wanted him to know that she cared. In tune with his mood and in time for his need. I love the touch of the word 'aforehand'. Sometimes our attempts come too late. We send our flowers to the grave—too late. Mary was in time, she came 'aforehand'.

Note finally **the servant rewarded.** The path of the servant is not an easy path. Think *how hurtful the murmurings were.* 'This waste,' they said criticising her deed. 'A beautiful deed,' was Christ's estimate. A different viewpoint brings a different verdict. It was told of Dr Guthrie that he met a small girl carrying her large, heavy baby brother along the street. 'That's a heavy burden you're carrying,' he said. 'It's no' a burden,' replied the little girl indignantly, 'it's ma brither!'

How grateful the Master was, and in his understanding and appreciation she had her reward. The appreciation was not only felt, it was 'telt'. What looks passed between Mary and the Master at that moment. Of grateful understanding from him, of adoring worship from her. On the death of a minister who had exercised very wonderfully the grace of appreciation, it was said 'there is no-one left to appreciate the little triumphs of little men'.

Top—Harvest thanksgiving, St George's-Tron Church, Glasgow

Bottom—Reflections on a highland loch

Nearly is Not Enough

Thou art not far from the kingdom
MARK 12:34

WHEN we were small we used to say sometimes to each other when the circumstances of our lives called for the remark—'nearly never killed a cat'. I don't know if the saying was purely a family one but whether that be so or not it illustrated a profound truth that it is never enough to be 'nearly' anything.

This is equally true in the spiritual realm and is illustrated most clearly in the incident in the gospels where our Lord says of a man 'Thou art not far from the kingdom of God'! 'Not far' but still not there. 'Nearly' never made a Christian might be the spiritual version of our childish saying.

I wonder if these words are being read by someone who is nearly a Christian. Let us look at this man in the gospels and note one or two things about him for our own good.

Note **the distance he had come.** When Christ said of him 'Thou art not far from the kingdom of God' he implied that in his mind and understanding of things this man had come a long way. This can be seen in *the appreciation the man showed* of the inwardness of the kingdom of God. 'To love God . . . is more than all whole burnt offerings.'

He showed here his understanding of the basic fact that Christianity depends on a relationship and not on ritual. But also this could be seen in *the aspiration the Master sensed* behind the question 'which is the *first* commandment . . .?' Here was a man who wanted to get to the heart of things. He was no trifler.

◀ The author in an autumn setting

F

Note also **the danger he was in.** He was not far but he was not there. He had come so far but not far enough. He was nearly there. There was the danger *of failing to take the final step*, of being content with being so near and the danger *of flinging away all the ground gained*, of losing all the worth of the progress so far made.

How much had been achieved, attained, and yet if the final step was not taken it would all be wasted. How tragic to throw away the results of years of prayer, of thought, of determination, and of preaching.

Note finally **the decision he must take.** To be not far required the decision to get in. How many there are who just need to take one more step to enter the kingdom of God. What does this step involve? First of all it involves *an acceptance of the King*. You cannot have a kingdom without a King, you cannot be a Christian without the Christ. So there must be an acceptance of his claims and his person. But this will lead to *an allegiance to the King*, with the understanding of the laws of the kingdom and the undertaking to live by these laws that this of course will mean.

May I end by asking you a question, are you 'nearly' a Christian, or are you a Christian? Are you not far from the kingdom of God, but still not there? If so why not take the final step and get into the kingdom, by receiving the King.

Saying . . . 'I will'

Wilt thou go with this man?

GENESIS 24:58

HOW many times I have faced a bride and bridegroom in a marriage service and waited for them to say the two short words that will change their relationship into that of husband and wife, 'I will'!

In the Old Testament is the story of the moment that came to a girl long ago when she too was asked to say 'I will'. It is one of the oldest love stories in existence and one of the loveliest. You will find it in Genesis 24, and it is well worth reading.

It is a perfect story in the pastoral setting of the Middle East, and in the perfection of its detail some have wondered whether or not there could be seen, in faint outline, the picture of God's love in its approach to the heart of man.

Read the story and note the concern of the father, Abraham, the activity of the servant, the waiting of the son, Isaac, the decision of the bride-to-be, Rebekah.

Is there here a prophecy in events of the parts of God the Father, God the Son and God the Holy Spirit, seeking in the church a bride for Christ? Let us take the story that way and see what the picture unfolds.

Note **the wealth with which love approaches.** The servant sets out laden with riches, and when he meets the one he feels to be the bride for his master's son, he gives her a golden earring and bracelets of gold, and then later he gave to Rebekah 'jewels of silver, jewels of gold and raiment . . . precious things'.

Is it not always so, that *love desires* to give? In every human relationship that is the hall-mark of love. Love gives, while lust takes. May we not expect to find then that God's love also desires to give? And so we find it, 'God so loved that he *gave* . . .' 'The *gift* of God is eternal life . . .' How utterly we wrong God when we make out that he is a thief, out to spoil and rob.

See too the servant unfolding all the wealth he has come to bestow. Love always delights in *the fullest display* of the worth of what it gives, not out of any motive of pride, but surely because only the best is good enough to give to the beloved.

Have you not known something of this display of love, as you have brought something choice and costly to give to the one you loved? How much more should not our God do the same for us? Think too of **the word for which love asks.** The servant had come for an answer, for a bride. Note *the urgency that showed*.

The matter was urgent and must be settled, and so the question was put to Rebekah. 'Wilt thou go with this man? And she said, I will go.' The word for which love waits and asks is the word of consent! Note *the authority that they sensed*.

In the story there was a recognition that God was in the matter (v. 50), just as we know perfectly well when God is dealing with us and that the issue is not a matter of argument with man but of answering to God.

There was the insistent request for a decision. The servant kept pressing for it, and was not content until he received it. Two tiny words, 'I will', that was all. Have you ever said the two tiny words to Christ?

Just a final glimpse at **the welcome with which love awaits.** On the night of Rebekah's return Isaac had gone out, as he had so often done, looking for her coming, and this night he saw her! How often he had gone only to see nothing, I don't know. But I can imagine *the expectancy with which love looked*. How long have you kept Christ waiting for you to come to him?

And what shall we say of the life that was to be shared by Isaac and Rebekah, *the intimacy to which love led*. But closer and deeper far is that bond which binds the soul to Christ, sharing the very life of Christ, in a happiness and usefulness that can only be known by those who have said their 'I will'. Have you said yours?

Always . . .

I do always those things that please my Father

JOHN 8:29

'ALWAYS' was the title of a popular song some years ago. 'I'll be loving you, *always*' was its theme. 'Always' also finds its place in the language of reproach or irritation, 'Why are you *always* late?' But in the Bible it can become part of the very stuff of Christian experience. There are certain things that ought to be found in every Christian life, everywhere and anywhere.

The Christian life truly lived means a life which is **always pleasing** to God; cf. John 8:29. 'I do *always* those things that please my Father.' What *a test this is to apply* to our programme of living. How far would you be able to say that what you do is 'always pleasing' to God?

This is after all the kind of test we were taught to apply in our early days; when we were not sure if a thing was right, we would check it with the thought 'would Mummy or Daddy like me to do this?'

What *a temptation to ignore* this simple rule, apply some other standard and do what is pleasing to ourselves or to the crowd. How much more challenging is this way of living than that which is so common and which merely takes its hat off to God in a greeting at church on Sunday morning.

The Christian life truly lived means a life in which we are **always praying** to God. This is the logical outcome of the first, and is found writ large in the New Testament. 'Praying always' is the background music of the testimony that rings out so clearly from the lips of New Testament Christians. If I am to live a life which

85

is always pleasing God there will have to be *constant reference to God*.

There will of course be the times when I am alone with God on my knees, but through the day there will be a constant reference to God of each situation as it arises. Surely this is what is meant by prayer. It is so much more than asking, it is submitting and discussing the tasks, problems and pleasures with our Father.

This demands a second thing, a *careful maintenance* of the lines of communication. Sin breaks contact with God, 'If I regard iniquity in my heart the Lord will not hear me'. If it is my desire to be always pleasing to God, then I must live a life in which I am always praying to God.

The Christian life so lived will lead to a life in which we are **always proving** God. There is a tremendous verse in 2 Corinthians 9:8. 'And God is able to make all grace abound toward you that ye, always having all sufficiency in all things, may abound to every good work' ' . . . always having all sufficiency.' That means, surely, always proving God's sufficiency! *How fearful we so often are*, afraid of the demands God may make, afraid of the difficulties we may meet.

But *how faithful God always is* . . . 'always having all sufficiency'. One of the mistakes we make is that we want to have grace in advance. We want grace today for tomorrow's needs, but God does not work that way. With the situation will come the sufficiency. The statement of the New Testament is 'My grace *is* sufficient for thee'; 'is', not 'will be' or 'may be'. Present grace for present need.

Finally, the Christian life thus lived is a life in which we shall be **always praising** God; cf. Philippians 4:4 'Rejoice in the Lord always and again I say rejoice.' *The theme of* our praise is 'in the Lord', *the thing* itself may or may not be pleasant but what God can do for us in that situation will bring the song to our lips.

Always pleasing . . . Always praying . . . Always proving . . . Always praising. Are these the kind of things you are 'always' doing?—they should be!

The Will of God and Me

Thy will be done
MATTHEW 6:10

WE see these words often on tombstones which suggests that they have to do with sickness and with death, whereas their context in the family prayer indicates that they have to do with life! 'Thy will be done on earth as it is in heaven.' I want to put it to you that the norm of Christian living lies in obedience to the will of God. A Christian is someone who does God's will moment by moment and day by day.

Doing the will of God is first of all **a matter of discernment.** If I am to do the will of God, then first of all I must know what that will is. In Colossians 1:9, Paul prays that they 'might be filled with the knowledge of his will in all wisdom and spiritual understanding'. I will soon become aware of the fact that *there are alternatives which challenge my allegiance* to the will of God. There is my own will which again and again must give way to his will.

How often we find Christ saying this, 'I came not to do my own will'. 'Not my will but thine be done', 'I seek not to do my own will but the will of my Father'. There is the will of the society in which I live, what is described in the New Testament as walking 'after the course of this world', doing what others do. There is the will of the devil, for we read of those who are 'taken captive by him at his will'.

There is further *the attitude which conditions my apprehension* of the will of God. In John 7:17 we read,

'If any man will do his will he shall know', or putting it another way, 'if we would know, we must first want to know'. I wonder how far the average Christian really wants to know the will of God, and if the reason why so few are doing it with real discernment is because so few really want to. We must begin here, if we are going to do the will of God; discernment is the first step.

Doing the will of God is also **a matter of commitment.** The words of the family prayer suggest that the will of God is not simply to be known, it is to be *done!* Discernment of it leads to commitment to it. This is not something merely theological but something intensely practical.

Think for a moment of *the sphere covered* by the will of God. In Colossians 4:12, Paul prays for the Christians at Colosse that they 'may stand perfect and complete in all the will of God'. The will of God was to be the atmosphere, the environment of the whole of their lives. We too are to live the will of God as if we were living in a country. Nothing is to lie outside the will of God. What we are, where we are, what we do, how we spend, what we say, the whole of life is affected by and related to the will of God.

Think also of *the standard created*—'on earth as it is in heaven'. How would the will of God be done in heaven? Surely it would be done and is done, eagerly, swiftly, steadfastly, thoroughly. This total re-orientation of life was grasped by Paul at the very hour of his conversion. Do you remember his cry, 'Lord what wilt thou have me to do?'

Doing the will of God is finally **a matter of enjoyment.** The fact that we find these words on tombstones suggest that we associate the will of God with the sad hours of life instead of the glad hours. But consider these words in Romans 12:2, 'That ye may prove what is that good and acceptable and perfect will of God'. We shall find in doing the will of God *that satisfaction for which love plans*. The perfect love of God will plan for our highest good and truest happiness; we can have no doubt about that.

But we must meet *the sacrifice for which love*

pleads. In order to prove the will of God, we must present ourselves a living sacrifice. But this is a principle of life at every turn. A girl will never know what marriage is unless she surrenders herself to the love that seeks it. A swimmer will never know the thrill of mastering the waves, unless he commits himself to them and forsakes the land. A student will never become a surgeon unless he surrenders himself to his work. A Christian will never know the will of God or do it or enjoy it until he surrenders himself to his Lord. Have you done that yet?

Friendship at Depth

Fellowship of the Spirit
PHILIPPIANS 2:1

THE Christian word for this quality of friendship is the word 'fellowship' and it opens the door to something of which the world is totally ignorant and thereby infinitely the poorer, something which is the glorious privilege of every Christian, born again of the Spirit. Ponder with me these thoughts.

The conditions that fellowship demands: Human friendship and Christian fellowship are both like plants, they will only flourish given certain conditions. There is no good complaining of their absence if we have not taken the trouble to fulfil these conditions.

The first condition is that of *the indwelling of the life of the Spirit of God*. 'The gift of the Holy Spirit' received by the individual by faith gives not only a new quality of life to that individual but also makes possible an entirely new relationship to others sharing the same gift. The whole wonderful experience of Christian fellowship is all made possible by the fact that we all share the same life. Just as in an ordinary family there is a close physical bond between the members of that family, so, in the family of God, there is a close spiritual bond.

This bond transcends so much that otherwise would separate and divide, social barriers, ecclesiastical, cultural, racial, intellectual—all these barriers are crossed and a blessed 'one-ness' is found. Of course what transcends also excludes, and those who have no share in the life find themselves 'outside' the fellowship.

The second condition is *the initiative of the love of the Spirit of God*. The coming of the life of the Spirit brings with it the constraint of the love of the Spirit, Romans 5:5, 'the love of God is shed abroad in our hearts by the Holy Spirit which is given to us'. If the love comes with the life then inaction is impossible to love.

Love must work, must think, must serve, must speak, must take the initiative and this outreach of love makes contact with the corresponding outreach from others motivated by the same love. So contact is made and communion or fellowship is begun.

The character that fellowship displays: 'There is a friend that sticketh closer than a brother' is the verdict of ancient wisdom. The first mark of true fellowship is *its depth*. What the book of wisdom is saying is that there is a deeper bond than that of blood. Every Christian will say Amen to that. However close the human ties are that bind us to each other in families, there is in what Paul calls 'the fellowship of the Spirit' a deeper and a stronger bond still.

What an answer this is to the fears that so many have when facing the cost of Christian discipleship. They are afraid that if they become Christians they will lose all their friends. The truth is that the friends they may lose cannot be compared to the friends they will gain.

The second characteristic of fellowship is *its delight*. In John 15:11 the purpose of fellowship is summed up in the phrase 'that your joy may be full'. Man is instinctively a social being and in no relationship does this instinct of the human personality find such fulfilment and satisfaction as in Christian fellowship. No Christian need ever be lonely. Every Christian should have a wide circle of friends.

Every Christian life ought thereby to be richer and happier than the non-Christian. The whole witness of such great gatherings of Christians as are found at Keswick, or Portstewart, or Filey is that the Christian life lived in the fellowship of the Spirit is a radiantly joyous thing.

The corrective that fellowship requires: We began by stating that fellowship is like a plant. We know that every plant has its pests. There are obviously *the perils that will spoil fellowship*. We find that fellowship can be selective and selfish, shallow and trivial. It can refuse to face the challenge of depth and obedience. Indeed one of the tragedies about so much so-called Christian experience is that there is so little of Christ in it.

But there is always *the place that will sweeten fellowship* between Christians and that is the place of fellowship with God himself. cf. 1 John 1:3, 4. 'That which we have seen and heard declare we unto you that ye also might have fellowship with us and truly our fellowship is with the Father and with the Son Jesus Christ.' The roots of a strong healthy fellowship are found here. May God grant that we may enter ever more deeply into this bond of 'fellowship in the Spirit', this experience of friendship at depth.

The Betrayal by Judas

. . . thirty pieces of silver
MATTHEW 26:15

AMONG the figures that move across the swiftly-changing series of events which culminated in the death and resurrection of Jesus Christ is the strange and enigmatical figure of Judas Iscariot—the man who sinned so greatly for so little. The sin of Judas lay in his betrayal of Christ. The strange and enigmatical aspect of it being that he betrayed him for so little, and yet, before we condemn Judas out of hand and think of him as a man apart, we would do well to look into our own hearts to see whether or not we ourselves are not sometimes guilty of the same supreme folly.

The thirty pieces of silver are mentioned three times and each time the attitude of Judas treats them so differently.

They were desired by him. In Matthew 26:15 we read of the agreement by Judas to betray him 'for thirty pieces of silver'. *How desperately Judas must have wanted them*, those thirty pieces of silver, and *how desperately he worked for them*, scheming and plotting in order to secure them.

Have we not discovered in our own hearts something of this? There has been something that we have desired and desired desperately? It has not been much, but we have wanted it and we have schemed and planned in order to secure it, even at the price of betraying our Lord. Yes, we too have known what it is to want so little so badly.

They were disdained by Judas. In Matthew 27:3 we read: 'When Judas saw that Christ was condemned, he repented himself, and brought again the

93

thirty pieces of silver, saying, I have sinned . . . and the chief priests said: "What is that to us?"'

How swiftly the silver has changed its value. Judas wanted it desperately and now he would give anything to be rid of it. An American preacher said once: 'How often sin lures us in anticipation only; how it dances before us like Salome before her uncle, Herod, quite irresistible in fascination. Happiness seems to depend on an evil deed.

'But how swift is the alteration in sin's aspect. It passes from anticipation through committal into memory and will never be beautiful again.' *The changed value* of the silver: we have known something of that, haven't we? We've got the thing we wanted so badly and find we do not want it any more. But even as Judas held the silver pieces in his hand *the contemptuous voices* of the Priests and Elders offered him no help in his dilemma.

They were discarded by Judas. In Matthew 27:5, we read: 'He cast down the pieces of silver in the temple and departed, and went and hanged himself.'

Consider *the forgotten factor*: the one thing Judas had overlooked is the one thing we can so easily overlook, too—the voice of conscience. Judas knew he had sinned and in the consciousness of that could not enjoy the fruits of it.

And consider, too, *the final folly*. Judas sinned, but so did Simon Peter; but how differently they acted after their sin. Peter had his sin dealt with by Christ, who forgave him, restored him, recommissioned him. Judas dealt with his sin by himself and went and hanged himself.

Thirty pieces of silver. So little, and yet wanted so badly.

May God grant to you and to me grace never to follow in the footsteps of Judas Iscariot 'which also betrayed him for thirty pieces of silver'.

Empty Conquest of Space

He that ruleth his spirit is better than . . .

PROVERBS 16:32

EVERY age has its conception of what constitutes greatness and arising out of that conception comes the conceit that can go with such greatness. At the time of the writing of the Book of Proverbs greatness was associated with military conquest. Today it would be the conquest of space. But just as every age has its conception of greatness, so it needs its corrective.

In Proverbs 16:32, we find this telling sentence: 'He that ruleth his spirit is better than he that taketh a city.' A modern version might run, 'He that controls his spirit is better than he that conquers space.' Sin is proving more difficult than space to conquer and modern man needs to be reminded of just this.

We live in a day when **the achievements of science are most impressive.** We live in *an age of wonder*. Man is probing further and further into space. Science has made rapid advances in the realm of medicine, although some 'progress' is creating new problems. So many exciting things have been brought into life by science, such as television; still to many of us an amazing thing. We are told that today 'brains must rule Britain, not blue blood'.

But we also live in *an age of worry*. Some of us are sufficiently aware of the fact that there are some of the most acute brains in the world ruling in the Soviet bloc, and we are sufficiently alert to realise that brains need to be rooted in character, and that character is more important than either brains or blue-blood! But the tragedy is that in this day when man's knowledge is more advanced than it has ever been, so man faces the direst peril and even his continued existence upon the earth is threatened.

We also live in an age when **the allurements of sin are most seductive.** Right from the beginning the devil has seen to it that sin is 'good for food, pleasant to the eyes, to be desired . . .' But never was there a time when *the pressure was so fierce.* At one time the home was the stronghold of religious faith and moral standards, but television has allowed the world to worm its way right into the very centre of the home life of every individual.

This has to be coupled to the fact that *the picture is so false.* In the affluent society in which we live more people have more money to spend and that therefore the numbers of those after that money has increased. In the meantime the mental attitudes of the nation are being unconsciously conditioned to accept the immoral as the normal.

One final thought; we live in an age when **the attainment of security is most elusive.** We face *the tragedy that baffles men.* Never before was there so much mental illness, nor has the divorce rate been so high. One preacher has said that congregations in America are so tensed up and strained that they cannot even go to sleep in church the way they used to do!

The root of the problem is to be found in that *treachery within that betrays men.* Man may be clever, but he is not good by nature. Man may be able to discern what is right but he desires what is wrong.

The remedy to the problem is found in the mastery from above that can redeem man. Man needs Jesus Christ to make him 'a new creature'.

Top—The Dome of the Rock, Jerusalem
Bottom—Dawn breaks at Leptokaria, Greece ▶

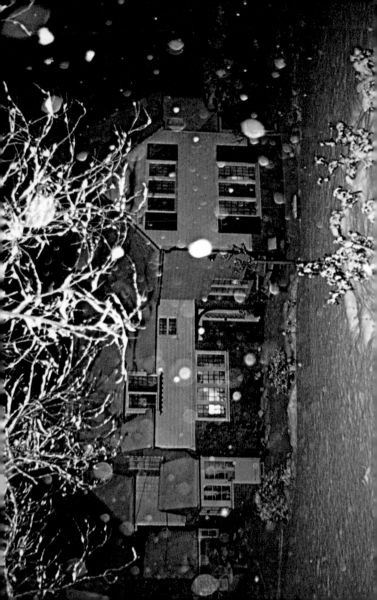

Rugged Living

In those days came John the Baptist . . .

MATTHEW 3:1

ONE of the most rugged and dramatic figures in the New Testament is that of John the Baptist. There are three things about him which we do well to consider.

Think of **the solitude he experienced.** Luke 1:80 says 'The child grew and waxed strong in spirit and was in the desert . . .' Here is a reflection, surely, of the loneliness of his spirit. Is it not the destiny of all great men that they experience a measure of isolation?

In this loneliness two things can be seen. *His communion with God.* It is no coincidence that we read 'he waxed strong in spirit . . . and was in the desert'. Greatness needs the divine strength born out of a life that spends much time in quiet with God. 'They that wait upon the Lord shall renew their strength' (Isaiah 40:31). Do we find a clue here as to why there is today a dearth of great men? Have we few powerful men because we have few praying men? *His contempt of the world.* His very dress and diet, 'camel's hair . . . locusts and wild honey', showed that here was a man who had rejected the scale of values commonly accepted. His disdain of the world's favour is seen in his fearlessness as he both exposed and rebuked the sin of his day.

Think also of **the silence he ended.** When asked who he was, John replied 'I am the voice of one crying'. Is there not a need for a casting out of a dumb spirit from the Christian for faith to become vocal? The first silence he broke was *the silence of toleration*; a new and yet old word, was heard again—'repent'. Repentance has been defined as 'the never again of an awakened soul'.

Judgment—God's judgment—against sin was proclaimed.

Toleration today is exalted into such a virtue that we are prepared to tolerate anything. We forget the divine intolerance of sin. We need people who will start calling dirt, dirt and sin, sin! *The silence of testimony* was also ended. For centuries the authentic voice of the prophet had not been heard—the 'thus saith the Lord'. At long last the silence was broken; the nation sensed it and the multitudes came. Is there any greater need today than for this—the authentic voice of God speaking through the church. If only that authentic voice could be heard again in the pulpits of our land.

Think finally of **the Saviour he exalted**. The true testimony of the New Testament is the same, 'we preach not ourselves but Christ Jesus . . .' *How clear his direction*. 'Behold the Lamb of God, which taketh away the sin of the world' (John 1:29). What a theme! To preach Christ. Is it any wonder that John felt unworthy of the task? 'One whose shoe latchet I am not worthy to stoop down and unloose.' But to point men to Christ was his privilege—and ours. *How costly his devotion*. How wonderfully was the nation aroused, and the figure who did it was John; his name was on everyone's lips. But having aroused the nation, having drawn the crowds, John had to see them leave him to follow Christ. 'He must increase and I must decrease' was his faithful and only comment. So John faded out of the picture again while Christ filled it. His work was done. It was well done.

What to do with Burdens

Blessed be the Lord our saving God who daily bears the burden of our life

PSALM 68:19 (Moffatt)

IT was surely by divine inspiration that John Bunyan introduces his pilgrim to us as a man with 'a great burden upon his back'. Nothing is more accurately descriptive of modern man in his more thoughtful moments. No words of Christ fall so appealingly upon the ears of men and women as 'Come unto me all ye that labour and are *heavy laden*'. So many people are carrying such heavy burdens that today more than half the beds in our hospitals are occupied by people who are not physically, but mentally or spiritually ill. What are we to do with our burdens?

There are **burdens to be shed.** We are not meant to carry them. They are too heavy to bear. It is of these burdens that the psalmist was thinking when he wrote the words quoted above. This finds an echo in the New Testament where in 1 Peter 5:7 we read the command 'casting all your care upon him for he careth for you'. Among the burdens to be shed: there is *the failure we face*. The burden of failure is one that we need not carry because God has chosen to do this in Christ. 'Who his own self bare our sins in his own body on the tree, that we being dead to sin should live unto righteousness' (1 Pet. 2:24). This is the 'good news' we hear through Christ.

There is also *the future we fear*. 'Casting all your care upon him, for he careth for you.' Casting is our part, caring is his! How many are loaded down with

99

fears, the possibilities that have to do with the future. We do this in spite of the explicit injunction of the Master himself 'Take no anxious thought, therefore, about tomorrow'. 'Therefore . . .' in the light of what has just been said—'your heavenly Father knoweth . . .' Add to the Father's knowledge, his love, grace and guidance, and what have we to fear!

Then there are **burdens to be shared.** 'Bear ye one another's burdens and so fulfil the law of Christ' (Gal. 6:2). The context suggests that Paul has in mind the failures and weaknesses of others that are to become our concern. Think *what a life may reveal.* Here is a life which has been overcome by the demands made upon it. This may be seen obviously or shared confidentially. Here is a life that has been misguided or deceived either through its own conceit or by the contrivings of others. Think again *what the law will require.* '. . . and so fulfil the law of Christ'. This is surely that law of Christ which is the law of love. Here is the obligation which the sympathy, the activity, the humility of love will seek to fulfil in a compassionate concern, to get under the burden of a life's, a world's need, and by the grace of God lift the burden in Christ's name.

Finally there are **burdens to be shouldered.** 'Every man shall bear his own burden . . . his own load of responsibility' (Gal. 6:5). This poses two questions, and the first is *For what am I responsible?* This responsibility must be assessed and then accepted. It will include and exclude. It will have to do with my family circle, business associations, the geographical location of my home and church, the personal gifts I have, the experience of spiritual grace I am given. The second question is *To whom am I responsible?* The answer: 'Everyone shall give account of himself to God' (Rom. 14:10).

Selected

By the three hundred men that lapped will I save you

JUDGES 7:7

IN every department of life we are familiar with the principle of selection whether it be a football team to play for a country or fruit to be displayed in a shop window.

In the realm of Christian service the same principle can be seen at work. In the Book of Judges we can see this illustrated in the story of Gideon and his three hundred. Read the story again in Judges, chapter seven.

We have here **a sifting of his well wishers:** in seeking deliverance for his people Gideon had declared war against the oppressors and summoned the nation to come to his help. Thirty-two thousand who wished him well had rallied in response! The cause of Jesus Christ too has never lacked well wishers; thousands of people have looked on at the efforts of the church and genuinely and sincerely wished her well. But mere well wishing seldom achieves anything.

The 32,000 followers were to be sifted out by two tests. The first was *the test of fearfulness*—'whosoever is fearful and afraid let him return', and 22,000 went! How much has never been attempted and therefore never achieved because of fear—afraid of failing, of what people would say, afraid it would be too difficult, afraid of not being able to keep it up?

The second test was *the test of casualness*. The ten thousand who remained were sifted still further and did not realise they were being tested. The potential army marched down to a stream. A mere handful paused momentarily for a quick cupped drink scooped up in the hand. The next got down to the business of drinking more thoroughly. It was hot, they were tired, there was plenty of time. They were casual and leisurely.

This same spirit is abroad today—what's all the hurry! Why be so keen! How many fail at the test of casualness—rejected and scarcely knowing it.

We have here also **a selection of his warriors,** a mere three hundred! Note firstly *the smallness of their number.* Only three hundred to tackle a vast army. But is it not true that God always works with a minority? Democracy needs a majority, Deity is content with a minority.

Let us never then be discouraged if we find ourselves in such company. Remember the three hundred of Gideon, the twelve of the Master, the two of Jonathan, and his words (1 Samuel 14:6), 'Come and let us go . . . it may be that the Lord will work for us: for there is no restraint to the Lord to save by many or by few.'

Note also *the eagerness of their nature.* While the nine thousand and seven hundred lolled and lay by the stream, the three hundred had crossed over and were half way up the other side of the valley!

Commenting on our Lord's words 'Seek ye first the Kingdom', Professor Henry Drummond addressed the students of his day with a blazing devotion 'seek it first, or leave it alone'. The warriors who take the cause of Jesus Christ to victory are those whose concern stamps their faith with both urgency and priority.

We have here finally **the strategy of his warfare** and the two points to note are this—firstly *how different his strategy was.* The issue was determined and settled not by swords but by trumpets, torches and shouts. It is so still. 'The weapons of our warfare are not carnal.' When will the Christian church accept the divine strategy—the weapon of prayer—the preaching of the word—the power and ministry of the Holy Spirit—the testimony of the believer.

Note *how decisive Gideon's strategy was*—in a night the vast might of a powerful enemy that for years had pillaged and robbed and enslaved a whole nation, was shattered. How powerful seem the forces arrayed against the church today—but cannot the omnipotent God deliver his people today as yesterday? The question for each of us to ask ourselves is this, where we do come into God's scheme, are we selected or rejected?

How Wise are You?

Four things which are . . . exceeding wise
PROVERBS 30:24

PROVERBS 30:24–28 speaks of 'four things which are little upon the earth but exceeding wise'—ants, conies, locusts and spiders.

The ants are wise because 'they prepare their meat in the summer'. They know that winter must come. Are we wise in recognising the *certainty* that summer will end? For many of us the freshness of youth has given way to the full glory of the summer time of growing maturity, but this will not last for ever. Autumn will soon be here, followed by the end of the year.

There are certain *opportunities* in life that don't return. It is a fact that not many people are converted to faith in Christ in old age. This would suggest that the earlier years offer the greatest opportunity. After summer the ways of life become rigid, the opportunity has gone.

The conies, or rock badgers, are wise because although they are but a feeble folk 'yet make they their houses in the rocks'. They have a fortress in which they are protected. How wise we are to recognise *the reality of the dangers* that confront us. How common is the folly of self-confidence? How many young people face life sure of their own wisdom, only to find the dangers too great?

So the conies find their deliverance in the rock. We too, should take refuge in the greater strength of our God, and find *our security from the dangers* that confront our lives. Like the psalmist in Psalm 62, we can say 'My soul waiteth upon God. He only is my rock and my salvation.'

The locusts are wise in that while they have no king 'yet go they forth all of them by bands'. *A single locust* is a harmless, defenceless insect, but a hoard of locusts is a force to be reckoned with. Sometimes one comes across people who say you can be a Christian without going to church. How can one be a wise Christian if you hold aloof from Christian fellowship? In Ecclesiastes 4:9, we read 'Two are better than one, if they fall the one will lift up his fellow'.

A swarm of locusts is a force to be reckoned with. The locusts go forth by bands, although they have no king. We who have such a King, surely will not forsake the assembling of ourselves.

It is not so easy to understand why the writer speaks of **the spider as being 'exceeding wise'.** 'The spider taketh hold with her hands, and is in kings' palaces.' But think of the spider's web. Its activity is *unseen*, but painstakingly perfect. If our lives were marked by this perfection, how wise we would be.

The wisdom of the spider lies also in its *unheeding* activity. 'The kings' palaces' mean nothing to the spider.

'A man's life consisteth not in the abundance of the things which he possesseth.' So how wise are you— or how foolish?

Place—Prominence— Pre-Eminence

That in all things he might have the pre-eminence
COLOSSIANS 1:18

SOMEONE has said that there are three kinds of Christians, those who give Christ a place in their lives, those who give Christ prominence in their lives and those who give Christ pre-eminence in their lives.

Those who give Christ place in their lives will be found on the membership roll of every church. Indeed it would be true to say that we have no right to be reckoned a member of the Christian church until we do give him place in our lives.

The action of such people is right. To give Christ room in our lives is absolutely right. This is what the Christ has desired. This is what so many of us have discovered. We know that the Christ of the New Testament church, of the twentieth century church is not simply the Christ of Galilee, not even just the Christ of the Cross, but the living, risen Christ in the heart. Discovering this we then have welcomed him and given him place and room in our lives.

The attitude of such people is wrong—if that is all that they or we have given to Christ. To receive him and then to ignore him is wrong. To have such a guest and then only to give him place is wrong. He should have so much more than that.

Those who give Christ prominence in their lives will be found in the life of every Church.

Such a people are *not ashamed to be Christ's*. He is given a prominent place in the arranging of their programme every week. When Sunday comes the thought never occurs to them of absenting themselves from divine worship. These folk are always found in the membership of the mid-week organisations. They will be found busy in the work of the fellowship. They will gladly accept office in the church or on its committees. They take a pride in all that their church stands for.

But Christ is *not allowed to be Lord* in such lives. There will be whole areas from which he is excluded. There will be reservations galore inserted in the terms of their discipleship. Like one of old they are constantly saying 'Lord, I will follow thee but . . .'

Those who give Christ pre-eminence in their lives are the heart of any living church. Like Paul their deepseated purpose is 'that in all things he might have the pre-eminence'.

How inclusive this ambition is—'in all things'; not in some, not even in most but 'in all'. There is no area from which he is excluded, no moment without his control.

How decisive this ambition is, for this is ultimately the kind of man the Holy Spirit can use. The first and supreme ministry of the Holy Spirit is to 'glorify Christ', and when the Holy Spirit finds a life with that very same intention, into that life he can and does come to make that life effective for God.

Three kinds of Christian—which kind are you?

In Full and Glad Surrender

Yield yourselves unto God

ROMANS 6:13

ONE of the most tremendous verses in the New Testament is 'Yield yourselves unto God, as those that are alive from the dead, and your members as instruments of righteousness unto God' (Rom. 6:13). It sounds like the demand the allies made when Germany sought terms of peace in world war II—unconditional surrender.

This is **surrender to a person**—'yield yourselves unto God'. Not to a creed, not to a church, but 'to God', a God we know in the face of Jesus Christ.

Note how *inclusive* is the gift, 'yield yourselves'. In that great hymn of consecration by Frances Ridley Havergal, 'Take my life and let it be consecrated Lord, to Thee', each verse amplifies this thought but the climax comes at the very end. . . . Take *my self!* To give one's self, is to give a gift which includes all. When our Lord was on earth a would-be disciple came to him with the words, 'Lord I will follow thee, but . . .' There are to be no 'buts' in this surrender.

It is also *decisive* 'Yield. . . .' The word is in the aorist tense, and that means something to be done once and for all. One modern translation puts it: 'Yield yourselves once and for all to God.' Has there ever been a moment in your life when you have thus yielded yourself to God?

This is also **surrender for a purpose.** '. . . and your members as instruments of righteousness unto God.' Phillips translates it, 'as weapons of God for his own purposes'. This postulates one question and answers another. The question it raises is this: *What are the intentions in the heart of God?*

They will be the intentions of one who is concerned with every man; the neighbour next door, the coloured folk of Africa, or the patients in the ward, for wherever there is man and wherever there is sin, the intentions of God are concerned with both righteousness and redemption.

How often men have asked 'Why doesn't God do something?' The question answered is: *What are the instruments in the hands of God?* Our text speaks of 'Your members as instruments . . .' God needs your members, your eyes through which to look with compassion, your lips to proclaim his love . . . your members! A doctor who was involved in a railway accident, walking up the line amid the wreckage, was heard to murmur bitterly, 'If only I had my instruments.' How often God must cry out for 'instruments'. Your members and mine are to be his instruments, and must be surrendered to him for this purpose.

But, finally, this is **surrender at a price.** 'Yield yourselves unto God as those that are alive from the dead' . . . as men living after death. There is *a loss to be faced.* Something akin to that of which our Lord spoke when he said . . . 'Except a corn of wheat fall into the ground and die, it abideth alone, but if it die it bringeth forth much fruit.'

But there is also *a life to be found.* We are to yield as those that are *alive* from the dead. This is something closely related to the surrender that every girl makes when she marries the man of her choice, there is a loss, there is so much that has to cease, her liberty, career, ambitions; but if there is loss there is such gain that she would never think of the loss!

Unconditional surrender! It seems a harsh demand in times of war, but in terms of love, it is just what we want and what love gives.

The Church and Our Cash

Now concerning the collection
1 CORINTHIANS 16:1

'THE church is always asking for money'—how often this is the kind of comment that can be heard. The church, of course, should never have to ask for money if the Christians in the church would give it. 'How do you raise the money you need?' was the question put to a pastor. 'We don't raise it, we give it,' was the reply.

It would do most British Christians a power of good if they were to visit the churches in the U.S.A., where the standard of giving makes our giving seem pathetic. The American Christians may earn more money but they don't earn that much more.

Paul laid down three principles to govern church giving. The Christian obligation to give should be **met regularly:** 'upon the first day of the week' is the counsel given in 1 Corinthians 16:2. *There is wisdom here:* Few of us can give large sums of money at any given time, but many small sums add up to a large total.

In the economic structure of industry calculations are sometimes made concerning the financial loss through absenteeism, in output and therefore in revenue. But what shall we say of the cost to the church of absenteeism.

Paul says we are to set aside what we plan to give upon the first day of the week—and surely that means every week, whether you are at church or not. *There would be wonder too* at the result if we obeyed the apostolic word here.

The Christian obligation to give should be **borne corporately:** 'Let every one of you.' *Everyone is to share* in this ministry—the privilege of it as well as the responsibility; if *everyone* did, then how much greater the total. But in this, alas, it is so often the case that never was so much owed by so many to so few. And each one is to share in this ministry.

No one is to be exempt.

The amount is not an issue yet in the mind of the apostle—the action is. There is no exemption permitted. However small, however large the gift, however poor, however rich the giver—each must give.

The Christian obligation to give will be **gauged proportionately** 'as God hath prospered him'. *Each will then give differently.* This is the New Testament principle, that comes back to the Old Testament tithe: the more I have to give, the more I am expected to give. A tenth from a rich Jew would be much more than a tenth from a poor Jew.

It will be so with the Christian. The rich will be expected to give much, much more than the poor. *Each will also give gratefully*, 'as God hath prospered him'. All that we have we owe to God, so we will not give grudgingly but gratefully.

If this is the New Testament standard of Christian liberality, how do you measure up to it? And how does your Church?

The Ministry of the Un-named

Behold, when ye are entered into the city, there shall a man meet you . . . he shall shew you a large upper room furnished . . .

LUKE 22:10–12

I FIND myself asking questions when I read of this incident—what man? . . . whose room? . . . whose hands had furnished it? And then I realise that I have stumbled across one of the facts true both of the New Testament and the whole history of the church since then, that a great deal of vital work is done by folk whose names are never heard—the ministry of the un-named. This starts a suggestive line of thought.

How frequently this ministry was relied upon. The boy with his fogotten lunch—the child taken up into the arms of the Saviour—the woman at the well of Sychar—the owner of the colt—the owner of the upper-room—how many there are whose names are never mentioned in the New Testament. This ministry of the un-named covers many lives and many services. As I pondered over it two further thoughts came to mind.

There was *never any doubt in the mind of Christ* that the service asked would be rendered. He said here in our text 'you will' not 'you may' find. The ministry of the un-named has a quality of reliability about it. How wonderful to be able to count on people without any doubt in our minds as to whether or not they would do what was expected of them!

There was *never any delay in the work of Christ*. The triumphal entry into Jerusalem was not postponed because there was no animal available for the Master. The Last Supper did not start late. This kind of secret service was therefore frequently relied upon and is still. I wonder if we are among those enlisted in its ranks.

How faithfully this ministry was rendered. I think there are two further things that can be said about this 'ministry of the un-named'.

There seems to have been *a willingness* about it. I don't get the impression that there was any reluctance, any hesitation. There were no excuses offered! There was a happy, glad, willingness. Is it not true that some service is rendered so grudgingly that all the pleasure is drained out of it? Have you ever had to say to a reluctant worker, 'Well, if that's how you feel about it, then don't do it'!

There seems to have been *a thoroughness* about it—'a large upper room furnished'. Was ever room prepared like this room? The mistress of the house would have been in and out of that room a hundred times during the day to make quite certain that everything that the Master could require was there. Thoroughness—what a wonderful quality this is.

How finally this ministry was rewarded. What was the reward that came the way of those who served in 'the ministry of the un-named'? It was not the reward that some seek, prominence for themselves in the annals of the church—an important position that kept them before the eyes of men—applause from the church. How often those who serve Christ do so to get just these very things. Instead we see two things.

The presence they secured was their reward. To them it was enough that they gained the presence of the Master they loved and whom they sought to serve. 'A large upper room furnished' that room would be for ever hallowed for them, just because he had been there.

The purpose they served: This was their reward, to have furthered the purposes of their Master, to have helped him. This unknown ministry draws its dignity, its meaning only from this one fact, it furthers the cause of the Master, of the Church of Jesus Christ.

The Ministry of the Un-named—are you in this? 'Great will your reward be' one day when the Master names you before angels and men.

The Coming One

Who was, and is, and is to come

REVELATION 1:4

ONE of the many names given to our Lord and Saviour Jesus Christ is that found in Revelation 1:4 which translated literally means 'the coming One'. What a perfect name that is for him. When we find ourselves approaching Christmas, we find ourselves in, what is called, the season of Advent, which is the name given to the beginning of the Church Calendar. So we do well to think through the significance of this name given to Christ as 'the coming One'.

The Christian who takes the Bible as the authority for what he believes reads there of **the Christ who did come.** Nearly two thousand years ago he came, when he was born in Bethlehem. That birth was a fulfilment of a prophecy spoken hundreds of years earlier by the prophet Micah in chapter 5 verse 2. 'But thou Bethlehem though thou be little among the thousands of Judah, yet out of thee shall he come forth that is to be ruler in Israel; whose goings forth have been from of old, from everlasting.'

When Herod the King heard of the quest of the Wise Men looking for a king who should be born whose star they had seen in the East, and asked the chief priests and scribes where Christ should be born, they knew the answer—Bethlehem! So it was to Bethlehem that the wise men came. Of what significance was that first coming to the world of the Christ.

To the Christian it speaks of *the proof of the loving of God*. Had there been no coming, then there would have been every justification for doubting if there could be any loving. The Bible states that God is love, the

Bible claims that 'God so loved the world that he gave'. Think of two at least of the qualities of love. Love is never content to remain unknown, love always seeks to reveal itself and that is part at least of the meaning of that first coming. 'The Word was made flesh and dwelt among us and we beheld his glory, the glory of the only begotten of the Father, full of grace and truth. Love, too, is never content to remain inactive. Love always wants to do something for or with the one loved, to give something to the one loved. At that first coming we see the love of God in action to meet man's deepest need, the need of a restored relationship with God through the forgiveness of man's sins. So we sing:

'Love came down at Christmas,
  Love all lovely, Love Divine,
  Love was born at Christmas,
  Stars and angels gave the sign.'

But the Christian also sees in that first coming *the price of the giving of God*. The first coming of Jesus was not only to Bethlehem, it was to Calvary. Right from the beginning Mary and Joseph knew that this child was destined to be the Saviour of the world, the message to Joseph was 'Thou shalt call his name Jesus for he shall save his people from their sins'. The gift that the love of God would give to men was a costly gift, though love would not have it otherwise! 'Ye were redeemed not with corruptible things such as silver and gold, but with the precious blood of Christ.'

But in the Bible we read also of **the Christ who still comes.** Calvary was not the end, for the Christ who died for the sins of the whole world, was raised from the dead and is alive for ever more. One of his most precious promises to his own before he left them was 'I will not leave you comfortless, I will come to you'. The One who had been with them physically, would come to dwell in them spiritually.

If we ask *why does he thus come to men?* the answer is simple enough for the Bible teaches that man is not only guilty but sinful. The need of man is more than the need of a new relationship with God, through the forgiveness of sins, man stands in need of new resources, because man is sinful. He needs more than pardon, he needs power. When the risen Christ faced the so-called church of Laodicea, he described that nominal church, as they were without Christ, as wretched, and miserable and poor and blind and naked! These words recall what he had quoted in the synagogue at the very beginning of his ministry, when he quoted the prophetic scriptures which described man as poor, brokenhearted, enslaved, blind and bruised! So he comes still to meet that need of men's hearts, and he stands at the door and knocks. 'I am come,' he had said, 'that they might have life and that they might have it more abundantly.'

If we ask *when does he then come to men?* the answer again is quite simple. He comes to dwell in the hearts and lives of men when he is trusted and invited so to do. Christ stands outside the life of a man waiting to be invited to come in. Just as simply as I would invite a friend to enter my home, so I can invite the Christ to enter my life. Does that sound too simple? Well, Jesus said the way would be simple! 'Except ye be converted and become as little children ye shall in no wise enter the kingdom of heaven.' To read some books by some preachers the impression one gathers is that before people can become Christians they need to become theologians! Christ said we had to become like little children! What a wonderful coming that is when I discover that he still comes. If you ask how do I know that he still comes, the answer is, 'because he said he would'.

But the Bible speaks of Christ in one other way, he is the coming One, because in the Bible we read of **the Christ who will come.** Here then is the climax to our understanding of Christ as 'the coming One'. He did come, he still comes, and he will come.' Why will he come again, visibly and personally as he said he would and as the angels said he would on the Mount of the Ascension, 'This same Jesus shall so come as ye have seen him go'?

The Bible indicates that there are at least two

reasons, the first is that he will come again *to complete a picture*, and that picture is the picture of himself. The prayer in the Anglican Prayer Book for the first Sunday in Advent speaks of his first coming as one 'in great humility', but at his second coming he is to come 'in his glorious majesty'. In his first coming he revealed himself as Saviour, in his second he will reveal himself as Sovereign Lord, before whom 'every knee shall bow'. At his first coming he came to save, at his second coming he comes to judge.

So that will mean also that he will come again *to conclude a story*, the story that went wrong when man sinned and rebelled against his creator. What a mess the sin of man has made of the world that God made for him, but the final word will be with God. There is coming a time of consummation, of separation, of restoration when there is to be 'a new heaven and a new earth'. My Father used to say that the story of the church began with a promise, 'This same Jesus shall come', and ends with a prayer 'Even so come Lord Jesus, come'. And faith says Amen to that, faith believes that Christ did come, still comes and will come. He is to faith, 'the coming One'.

God Has His Man for His Hour

For such a time as this
ESTHER 4:14

HISTORY as well as the Bible bears witness to the fact that God has his man or his woman for his hour. One book of the Bible which illustrates this better than most is the Book of Esther, and yet the strange fact is that though the hand of God is seen at work throughout the book, the name of God is never mentioned.

Let us look at the central figure in the book, Esther, the young and lovely woman upon whom the fate of a nation was to hang.

Let us note **how comfortably she lived.** Two things would characterise her way of life. There was *the affluence she enjoyed.* After all, was she not Queen of one of the greatest empires the world had ever known. Her every want would be supplied. Enrichment was here, beyond her wildest dreams. Is there not a correspondence here to note with the life so many of us live—enrichment, whether spiritually or materially, has been ours.

I note also the *ignorance she exhibited.* How close to disaster she was living. Beyond the palace walls, within the palace itself, forces were at work planning to destroy her people and herself. Tell me, are there not similar forces at work today, the existence of which we ignore at our peril.

Let us note also **how courageously she ventured.** Into this comfortable way of life came the wind of change. The truth broke with shattering effect.

I see *a summons she was asked to obey;* a message came charging her that she should 'go in unto the king for her people'. She was asked to recognise that the sphere of influence into which she had been brought was to be used for others and for God. So it always is.

I see also the *sacrifice she was asked to make.* To obey was to risk the loss of all she had, the comfort she enjoyed. This she proved willing to do. 'If I perish, I perish.' How desperate the venture; how courageous the spirit. Is there not a need today for such an upheaval in the soft, indulgent pattern of life so many Christians enjoy.

Let us note finally **how completely she triumphed.** It is the old story of God using the weak things of the world to confound the mighty.

We see *the signs of God's presence* as the story unfolds. We are conscious that an advising hand is over-ruling the development of events. God's servants never work alone. They are 'workers together with God', and so this lovely girl becomes the instrument of God's deliverance.

No wonder the story ends with *the songs of God's people.* When news of their deliverance spread 'the city of Shushan rejoiced and was glad'. 'Wilt thou not revive us again that thy people may rejoice in thee?' is the cry of the human heart. What songs are there like the songs of deliverance? How we need to hear these songs again today.

The Mother of our Lord

Blessed art thou among women
LUKE 1:28

THERE is a tendency within the reformed and protestant churches to overlook the part that Mary played in God's plan of redemption. This is understandable when one faces the exaggeration of her part that marks another section of the Christian church.

A girl was recently in hospital with a serious and long illness. It was a hospital run by the Roman church, and frequent services were held in the ward, but the girl couldn't help noticing that the services were always held around the statue and picture of the Virgin Mary and the statue and picture of her Son at the other side of the ward were left deserted.

That section of the church would do well to recall the words of Mary herself concerning her Son, 'Whatsoever *he* saith unto you do it.' Or to have the mind of the saintly old minister who entered one of the homes in his parish to find it was a Roman home. The woman who greeted him saw him looking at the pictures of the Virgin that adorned the mantlepiece and said, 'She was a wonderful woman' to which he replied gently, 'And she had a wonderful Son!'

But there are lessons for us to learn as we consider Mary's part, for in the wonderful story of her experience we can see reflected something of the wonder that marks the experience of every Christian.

Think of **the message that came to Mary** to unfold the purpose of God for her. Spiritual experience still involves messengers, the messenger may be the mother, the Sunday School teacher, the vicar, the

120

evangelist, the broadcaster, or the Christian friend, but still God uses messengers in his work.

There was *a recognition by Mary* of his presence and person. In Luke 1:26–29, we read: 'when she saw him', she saw and recognised the messenger as one sent from God. She recognised him for what he was, the messenger of God to her soul. And so it is with us, deep down, although the messenger is no angelic being, we too recognise the source and authority of the message that he brings.

What of *the reaction of Mary?* Her reaction was very like our own, 'she was troubled'. Why is it that so often the reaction in the human heart to an awakening to the fact of God, the truth of God, the presence and purpose of God, is so often one of fear? Is it because of the truth that we feel he knows, about us? Is it because of the threat we believe he is to our happiness?

Think further of **the message that challenged Mary.** A strange and wonderful message it was. We find it in vv. 30–35 of the same chapter. What shall we say of *the dignity it conferred* upon her. 'Highly favoured' she was indeed, to be called of God to bear in her body the Christ of God, to share in the mystery and miracle of his birth. Out of all the women in history she was the chosen one for this high purpose.

But as great a dignity is still ours in the message of God's desire for us. It is essentially similar, that our bodies should become the temple and dwelling place of the risen Christ. What a dignity is ours.

But note *the difficulty it created.* When the full wonder of God's purpose for her broke in upon her soul, Mary's response was so much like our response, 'How can this be?' And the answer to Mary's problem and ours is one and the same, by 'the Holy Ghost'. What mystery, what miracle is here, that the life of the risen Lord is ours by the Holy Spirit.

My last thought then is of **the miracle that changed Mary.** Think of *the submission of her will* that enabled the miracle to be wrought! Listen to her response. 'Behold the handmaid of the Lord, be it unto me according to thy word.' Was ever submission so complete as this? It was a submission that set no limit to what God might ask or do. Have we ever given such a submission as this to the will of God?

But the final note in the miracle that changed her was in *the sweetness of her name* that resulted from the miracle. 'All generations shall call me blessed' so she sang in the joy that filled her soul, and indeed they have and do still call her blessed. And the name of the village maiden that might have been lost in the obscurities of an eastern village of long ago has been hallowed and loved all down the centuries ever since.

It can be even so with us, for God still delights to take those who are simple and ordinary, and so work in their lives the miracles of his grace and power that countless lives rise up to call them blessed. Has the miracle that changed Mary changed you?

Treasure Hunt

Where is he . . .? we have seen his star
MATTHEW 2:2

DECEMBER is the month of Christmas parties, which bring excitement to the children and a host of memories to the older folk. Among my own memories, one of the most vivid is that of the treasure hunts that were always part of the programme at one home.

That children's game is, however, a parable, and I want to link it up with the first treasure hunt that I know of, which is associated with Christmas; the story of the wise men and their search for the Christ of Bethlehem. I think that we shall find in it a picture of the kind of search that many of us still make before we too find the Christ.

Think first of all of **the search they made.** It was long, facing many difficulties, and it all started with no greater light than that of a single star. In the parties of my childhood it was like that; sometimes just a faint clue as to where the treasure might be found and then a long search.

So it is sometimes with the soul. Not always, for some find their way quickly to Christ after some shattering revelation of God, like the shepherds whose feet hastened to where the child lay.

For others the finding of Christ is a quiet, hidden experience of God's power at work in their lives, like that of Mary herself. But to others it is the way of the long weary search, following the glimmer of a single light that holds the promise that God is, and that Christ can be found.

The light may be the life of a Christian whose life bears testimony to the fact of God; it may be a text which sticks in the mind and seems to hold the promise of something beyond the words, something which is alive; it may be the memory of an experience of long ago that still lights up the inner recesses of the soul with its flickering gleam. That star held them to their quest, and on they journeyed.

Then note **the truth they heard.** Sometimes at those parties one of the grown-ups would take pity on me and give a hint as to where my own particular treasure might be found. It was so with the wise men. They had searched long and at last came to Jerusalem and there, when they sought for guidance, it came to them from the pages of the word.

It is a great thing when, in our quest for God and Christ, we are directed to what the Word of God has to say. There is such a danger that we take our guidance from the imaginings of our own mind, or from the uninstructed opinions of our friends. If there is someone reading these words and you have so far not found Christ in a living personal way, then may I urge that you turn to the Word of God, and read through one of the gospels, thoughtfully, honestly and unhurriedly. You will be told there where and how Christ is to be found.

The third thing I note in this story is **the assurance they got.** We read in that second chapter of Matthew's Gospel, that 'the star went before them till it came and *stood over where the young child was*. When they saw the star they rejoiced'.

They knew that they were 'getting warm', they were nearing the end of their quest.

Do you have memories of your childhood when you were told that you were getting warm? When you knew that you were not far from the treasure you sought! I think it is true to say that many people in their quest for Christ know something about this.

They are finding a real measure of enjoyment in the services of the church, in the company of other Christians. They are not themselves Christian, they know, but their expectancy is real. They know that Christ is to be found. The light seems to be centring round one particular fact, they are no longer looking everywhere, anywhere.

The last thought is that of **the Redeemer they found.** 'When they were come into the house, they saw the child.' Can something of the thrill of your finding your treasure as a small child, can something of that wonderful moment kindle your heart afresh? It was wonderful, to reach under that cushion and to feel the crinkly paper, to pull out the parcel with your name on it. The excitement of tearing the paper off and then the treasure was in your hands.

Happy memories! But how much more wonderful the day when we find Christ, when after the long search, lasting over weeks or months, we find ourselves brought face to face with the reality of a living Lord, when we make the discovery that the Christ of long ago, the Christ of Bethlehem, of Calvary, is alive today and that he waits to enter the heart that is opened to receive him.

That is a moment indeed when in full consciousness of our utter unworthiness, but with a great desire to know his grace and help, we ask him to come in and by his Holy Spirit, to be our personal Saviour and Lord.

Holy Jesus, Mary's Child,
  Make thee a bed, soft, undefiled
Within my heart, that it may be
  A quiet chamber, kept for thee.

'They saw the Child . . . *and worshipped him*.'

What's Your Ambition

That I may know him . . .
PHILIPPIANS 3:10

I WONDER if you have any clear cut ambition governing your outlook and outreach as a Christian? We must all have heard the well-worn cliche 'the person who aims at nothing hits it'. So many Christians seem to have absolutely no idea what they are looking for in their Christian lives.

I want to look with you at one verse which almost casually reveals the three things upon which the ambition of Paul was centred. You will find them in Philippians 3:10 'That I may know him and the power of his resurrection and the fellowship of his sufferings.' I wonder if I would find in your heart what I find in Paul's heart.

We see here **the priority of the person of Christ in his life.** 'That I may know him . . .' Paul was concerned supremely with Jesus Christ. He wants to know him above everything else. If this ambition was to be realised then two things would be related to this ambition.

There would be *the truth to be discovered about Christ.* This would take time and thought. And yet, how much time are you and I prepared to give to getting to know Jesus Christ through his word? This is the best way to get to know him although of course we will learn about him from others, but most of all when we are alone with his word!

There would also be *the trust to be deepened in Christ.* Most of us are trying to trust a Lord we do not really know. This is stupid. 'Faith cometh by hearing and hearing by the word of God.'

We see also here that Paul was concerned with **the necessity of the power of Christ to meet his need.** To know Christ, to trust Christ, meant to obey Christ, and this is possibly the most challenging thing about being a genuine Christian. We realise that we must obey Christ before we think of obeying the crowd or even of satisfying our own desires.

Paul was *alert to the standard demanded by Christ.* It is a high standard, so high that it seemed impossible. The Christian life is never content with anything less than the best, God's best. But Paul was also *alive to the supply provided in Christ,* 'the power of his resurrection . . . of his risen life'. What God required, God provided. What kind of standard have you set yourself? Paul did not shrink from the highest.

We see finally here that Paul was concerned with **the identity with the purpose of Christ in his heart.** Paul was not united to his risen Lord either for fun or for his own comfort but so that he might with his Lord seek to work out the purposes in the heart of that Lord. '. . . the fellowship of his sufferings.'

Christ's sufferings were vicarious, they were voluntary. Christ got under the burden of a world's sin and lifted the load to set men free. Paul wanted to identify himself with that purpose. Do you?

Think of *the compassion in the heart of Christ.* He cared for others. He loved the world! Think of *the compulsion in the heart of Paul.* With the life of Christ there had come the love of Christ which 'constrained him'. Three ambitions found in the heart of a great Christian. Are they found in your heart and mine? If not—why not?